The Fundamentals of
DRAWING
TECHNIQUES

The Fundamentals of
DRAWING TECHNIQUES

A PRACTICAL COURSE FOR ARTISTS

Barrington Barber

ARCTURUS

ARCTURUS

This edition published in 2011 by Arcturus Publishing Limited
26/27 Bickels Yard, 151–153 Bermondsey Street,
London SE1 3HA

Previously published as *Advanced Drawing Skills*
Copyright © 2003 Arcturus Publishing Limited/Barrington Barber.

ISBN: 978-1-84873-818-6
AD000019EN

Printed in Singapore

Contents

Introduction

To get the most out of this book, you will need to be familiar with the basic drawing practices I introduced in *The Fundamentals of Drawing*. If you have used that book, or feel you know enough without referring to it, welcome to the next interesting stage of drawing. Although we use the term 'advanced' in the title, the book is aimed not at professionals but at still-aspiring artists who have done a lot of work and want to develop their skills further.

If you are still using the exercises in the last book as practice tools, that's very commendable. In this book, I aim to encourage you to look more deeply into the art of drawing and to bring a more investigative approach to what you do. Such an approach teaches us not to be put off by difficulties, because they can be overcome with a little persistence and a lot of practice. If you are now drawing quite well and have proved your ability to yourself, it is quite easy to improve, even if the further steps you must take appear to be difficult at first.

So, the first lesson of this book echoes recurring themes of the last: practise regularly, and don't mind making mistakes in the process. Mistakes are not bad so long as you correct them as soon as you see them. You will find that assessing your ability will help to make you more objective about your work. However, this new knowledge won't happen overnight, so be patient. And remember: the time you spend altering your drawings to improve them is never lost – that is how you will improve your skills.

Making contact with other people who are also trying to become better artists will help your progress, too. Drawing is not a private exercise but a public one, so do show your work to other people. It may not be to everybody's liking and you may have to swallow criticisms that dent your pride. If this happens, look at your own work again with a more objective eye and see if those criticisms are justified. Of course, not all criticism is correct. But usually we know when it is, and when it is we should act on it. Your best critics will be other students of art because they speak from their own experience. If you know any professional artists, talk to them about their work. You will find their advice useful. Go to art shows and galleries as often as you can and see what the competition is up to. The experience will help to push your work further in the right direction. Notice your own weaknesses, try to correct them, but don't ignore your strengths. And while you build on success, try to eliminate the gaps in your knowledge and expertise. Above all, don't give up. Steady hard work often accomplishes more than talent.

WHAT YOU WILL DISCOVER

In the following sections we will be looking at all sorts of drawing; some you will be familiar with, and some will be new to you. Many of my examples are close copies of the work of first-rate artists, who provide a wealth of ideas and methods that can be learnt from. Some of the drawings are my own and hopefully they will also teach you something. In considering the drawings of master artists and how they were done, I have tried to relate them to our experience of drawing and suggest ways of improving your abilities.

Topics such as anatomy and perspective are looked at in some detail, as is the difficulty of drawing movement. Detailed on the facing page are the major themes running through the book and how they can help you develop your drawing skills. Included in this Introduction also, just as a taster, are examples of drawings that exemplify the major topics we shall explore.

Line and style: The loose and yet taut line evident in the copy of Matisse odalisque (below) can take years to perfect, but there is no reason why you should not try to produce something similar now – it will enormously improve your drawing skills.

A vivid sense of style can make even a line drawing stand out. The simple, refined but original design of this cut out bronze figure from the Hellenic period (right) is first class. Once we have seen drawing of this calibre we can begin to emulate it.

Different approaches: Careful refined pencil drawing (left), a copy of a Michelangelo; and an immediate and unpremeditated drawing in pen, line and wash, original by Guercino.

Major Themes:

- Form and how to produce an effect of dimension, with shapes conditioned by light and shade and other dimensional devices – see pages 79–109.

- Devices and approaches that may help us to improve the accuracy of our drawing (see pages 48–77). We'll also consider how to analyse the mass of information thrown at our retina.

- Ways of portraying an emotional state or mood in a picture – see pages 111–125. This is done by the design, the choice of subject matter, or by the techniques and drawing medium. All work and all are valid.

- Studying from nature – see pages 127–163. In this and other sections you will find exercises in drawing and analysis, to understand how to see a subject more clearly and how to represent what you see.

- Caricature – see pages 165–75. Although this is not a major part of art it does encapsulate the sharp vision that an artist needs in order to see past the obvious. There is a lot beyond our daily perception.

- The work of artists who found ways of seeing the world anew – see pages 15–45. In their hands what might seem an ordinary situation suddenly becomes full of promise and life.

- The importance of drawing what you *can* see. Not to draw what can't be seen might seem obvious, but it is a very precise discipline for the artist with lots of ideas in his head who sometimes attempts to invent without substance. It's easier – and the end result more convincing – to train yourself to see more, perceive more clearly and draw exactly what is seen. Anyway try it out. You might be surprised.

HOW YOU WILL LEARN

It is hoped you will have a great time with the suggestions in this book. Having taught art now for a long time – and practised it even longer – I can say with confidence that if you want to learn to draw well there is nothing to stop you.

Some of the styles and techniques will suit you instantly whereas with others you may find yourself having to work hard. Don't worry if you don't instantly get on with some of them. See them as a challenge to your obvious intelligence; if you want to draw, you must be very intelligent, no matter what your academic record. You will discover that just trying a new technique will bring improvement in the other methods you use. Seemingly difficult exercises firm up our talent. When you succeed at them, give yourself a pat on the back, because it means you are really getting interested. That, ultimately, is what counts, and what improves levels of skill.

Above all, remember that your own will and desire to draw and the normal use of your senses are all that are required to start the deeper investigation into the visual world that this book hopes to encourage. Art is a marvellous part of life, and drawing is the real basis for painting and sculpture. The more deeply you engage in the arts, the more you are adding to the cultural value of our society.

Different effects with chalk: Both of these drawings are in the classical manner, but notice how different they look. In the copy of the Vouet (left) the carefully modulated toning makes us very aware of the aesthetic value.

In the copy of the Caracci (right) you can see that it was drawn quickly. Most of the tonal lines go in the same direction and the figure looks solid and convincingly muscular.

Different effects with brush and ink: These two landscapes give very different effects although a very similar technique was used for both.

DRAWING YOUR WORLD

Before we begin, I would like you to bear in mind a few points that I hope will stay with you beyond the period it takes you to absorb the contents of this book. It concerns methods of practice and good habits.

One invaluable practice is to draw regularly from life. That is, drawing the objects, people, landscapes and details around you. These have an energy and atmosphere that only personal engagement with them can capture. Photographs or other representations are inadequate substitutes and should only be used as a last resort as reference (see top caption on opposite page).

Always have a sketch-book or two and use them as often as possible. Constant sketching will sharpen your drawing skills and keep them honed. Collect plenty of materials and tools – pencils, pens, rubbers, sharpeners, ink, paper of all sorts – and invest in a portfolio to keep all your drawings in.

Keep a sketch-pad always with you – you never know when you'll stumble across a scene that you want to put down on paper.

These quick sketches of different parts of buildings are the result of drawing often and at any time. There is always the possibility of making a sketch of something seen out of a window. It's very good practice, too.

Don't throw away your drawings for at least a year after you've finished them. At that distance you can be more objective about their merits or failings, and have a clear idea of which ones work and which ones don't. In the white-hot creative moment you don't actually know whether what you've done is any good or not. You are too attached to your end result. Later on you'll be more detached and be clearer in your judgement.

Build a portfolio of work and sometimes mount your drawings. Then, if anyone wants to see your work, you will have something to show them. Don't be afraid of letting people see what you have done. In my experience, people always find drawings interesting. Have fun with what you are doing, and enjoy your investigations of the visual world.

When drawing from life is not possible, use your own photographs of objects or scenes of interest. This is better than relying on other people's shots, because invariably your visual record will remind you of what it was about that image you wanted to capture.

One of the most important lessons I hope you will take from this book is the value of simplicity. Successful drawing does not demand a sophisticated or complex approach. Look at this sketch. Its quality derives from a simple approach to shapes and the assimilation of their graphic effects into one picture. I had to make an effort to keep those shapes basic and simple. Always try to do the same in your drawings.

Drawing from the Masters

The point of this section is not to encourage you to blindly copy the methods of Raphael or Leonardo or any of the other great masters whose works we'll be looking at. The most important aspect of drawing of this quality is the acute observation that it requires. Great artists observe the world around them with great accuracy. I have deliberately not provided captions for the images reproduced here, because I want you to regard this section as an exercise in looking.

From these examples I want you to begin to understand how to put technique at the service of your observations by varying the length and pressure of your strokes. Eventually, after a lot of practice, you will find that you can judge exactly how heavy, light, long or short your strokes should be to achieve a specific effect. Hopefully, you'll also find that you can get quite fast at it.

One of the great bonuses of studying drawing and painting is that our vision refines and we begin to drop the prejudices and preconceptions that normally accompany our view of the world – attributes that are abundantly in evidence in the work of the artists whose methods we look at in this section.

ANCIENT GREEK ART

These Greek vase drawings, some of the earliest known (dating from c. 510 BC), are so sophisticated and elegant they might have been drawn by a modern-day Picasso or Matisse, except that Matisse would not have been as exact and Picasso would probably not have been as anatomically correct. The simple incised line appears to have been done easily and quickly and yet must have been the result of years of practice. Yet more remarkable is that these drawings were not done on flat paper but on the curving surface of a vase or crater. The economy of line is a lesson to all aspiring artists.

LEONARDO DA VINCI (1459–1519)

When we look at a Leonardo drawing we see the immense talent of an artist who could not only see more clearly than most of us, but also had the technical ability to express it on paper. We see the ease of the strokes of silverpoint or chalk outlining the various parts of the design, some sharply defined and others soft and in multiple marks that give the impression of the surface moving around the shape and disappearing from view.

Leonardo regulates light and shade by means of his famous *sfumato* method (Italian for 'evaporated'), a technique by which an effect of depth and volume is achieved by the use of dark, misty tones. The careful grading of the dark, smudgy marks helps us to see how the graduations of tone give the appearance of three dimensions.

The effect of dimension is also shown with very closely drawn lines that appear as a surface, and are so smoothly, evenly drawn that our eyes are convinced. There is elegance in the way he puts in enough tone but never too much. To arrive at this level of expertise requires endless practice. However it is worth persevering with practising techniques because they enable you to produce what you want with greater ease. Techniques need to be mastered and then forgotten. All this will take time.

RAPHAEL (RAFFAELO SANZIO) (1483–1520)

The perfection of Raphael's drawings must have seemed quite extraordinary to his contemporaries, even though they had already seen the works of Filippo Lippi, Botticelli, Michelangelo and Leonardo. His exquisitely flowing lines show his mastery as a draughtsman; notice the apparent ease with which he outlines the forms of his Madonna and Child, and how few lines he needs to show form, movement and even the emotional quality of the figures he draws. His loosely drawn lines describe a lot more than we notice at first glance. It is well worth trying to copy his simplicity, even though your attempts may fall far short of the original. The originals are unrepeatable, and it is only by studying them at first hand you will begin to understand exactly how his handling of line and tone is achieved.

MICHELANGELO BUONARROTI (1475–1564)

Michelangelo is arguably the most influential figure in the history of art. Study his drawings and then look at the work of his contemporaries and the artists who followed him and you will see how great was his influence. The copies shown here incorporate the original techniques he introduced. In the pen and ink drawing the style is very free and the shapes very basic, suggesting figures in motion; the ink drawing with traces of chalk is still pretty sketchy but more considered, allowing the viewer to discern character and type of costume. The final example is a very exact drawing, the careful *sfumato* in black chalk giving a clear definition of the arrangement of the flexing muscles under the skin. Michelangelo's deep knowledge of anatomy enabled him to produce an almost tactile effect in his life drawing. He shows clearly that there are no real hollows in the human form, merely dips between the mounds of muscles. This is worth noting by any student drawing from life and will give more conviction to your drawing.

PETER PAUL RUBENS (1577–1640)
Now let us look at the beautiful
delicately drawn chalk drawings of
Rubens who, like Titian, was referred to
as a prince of painters. Before he
produced his rich, flowing paintings,
full of bravura and baroque asymmetry,
he would make many informative
sketches to clarify his composition.
These sketches are soft and realistic,
with the faintest of marks in some areas
and precise modelling in others.

The rather gentle touch of the
chalk belies the powerful composition
of the figures. When completed the
paintings were full and rich in form. His
understanding of when to add
emphasis and when to allow the
slightest marks to do the work is
masterly.

Rubens was one of the first
landscape painters, although he did
this type of work only for his own
satisfaction. His drawings of landscapes
and plants are as carefully worked out
and detailed as those of any Victorian
topographical artist.

HANS HOLBEIN THE YOUNGER (1497/8–1543)

Holbein left behind some extraordinarily subtle portrait drawings of various courtiers whom he painted during his time as court painter to Henry VIII. These works are now in the Queen's Collection (most of them at Windsor, but some are in the Queen's Gallery at Buckingham Palace), and are worth studying for their brilliant subtle modelling. These subjects have no wrinkles to hang their character on, and their portraits are like those of children, with very little to show other than the shape of the head, the eyes, nostrils, mouth and hair. Holbein has achieved this quality by drastically reducing the modelling of the form and putting in just enough information to make the eye accept his untouched areas as the surfaces of the face. We tend to see what we expect to see. A good artist uses this to his advantage. So, less is more.

REMBRANDT (HARMENSZ VAN RIJN) (1606–69)

The drawings of Rembrandt probably embody all the qualities that any modern artist would wish to possess. His quick sketches are dashing, evocative and capture a fleeting action or emotion with enormous skill. His more careful drawings are like architecture, with every part of the structure clear and working one hundred per cent. Notice how his line varies with intention, sometimes putting in the least possible and at other times leaving nothing to chance. What tremendous skill!

To emulate Rembrandt we have to carefully consider how he has constructed his drawings. In some of his drawings the loose trailing line, with apparently vague markings to build up the form, are in fact the result of very clear and accurate observation. The dashing marks in some of his other, quicker sketches show exactly what is most necessary to get across the form and movement of the subject. Lots of practice is needed to achieve this level of draughtsmanship.

GIOVANNI BATTISTA TIEPOLO
(1696–1770)
Tiepolo is noted for his painted walls and, particularly, ceilings. Although difficult to emulate, his methods of drawing are worth studying. Loose, scrawling lines are accompanied by splashes of wash to give them solidity. What appear to be little more than scribbles add up to wonderful examples of a master draughtsman's first thoughts on a painting. Compare his drawings closely with his elegant paintings and you will see premonitions of the latter in the former.

JEAN-ANTOINE WATTEAU (1684–1721)

One of the most superb draughtsmen among the French artists of the 18th century, Watteau painted remarkable scenes of bourgeois and aristocratic life. His expertise is evident in the elegant and apparently easily drawn figures he drew from life. When we look at them, it seems that somehow we can already draw like this or perhaps that we never shall.

Like all great artists he learnt his craft well. We too can learn to imitate his brilliantly simple, flowing lines and the loose but accurate handling of tonal areas. Notice how he gives just enough information to infer a lot more than is actually drawn. His understanding of natural, relaxed movement is beautifully seen. You get the feeling that these are real people. He manages to catch them at just the right point, where the movement is balanced but dynamic. He must have had models posing for him, yet somehow he infers the next movement, as though the figures were sketched quickly, caught in transition. Many of his drawings were used to produce paintings from.

JEAN-AUGUSTE-DOMINIQUE INGRES (1780–1867)

Ingres was, like Raphael, noted for his draughtsmanship. His drawings are perfect even when unfinished, having a precision about them which is unusual. He is thought to have made extensive use of the camera lucida (see page 51), which is probably correct, but nevertheless the final result is exceptional by any standards.

The incisive elegance of his line and the beautifully modulated tonal shading produce drawings that are as convincing as photographs. Unlike Watteau's, his figures never appear to be moving, but are held still and poised in an endless moment.

The student who would like to emulate this type of drawing could very well draw from photographs to start with, and when this practice has begun to produce a consistently convincing effect, then try using a live model. The model would have to be prepared to sit for a lengthy period, however, because this type of drawing can't be hurried. The elegance of Ingres was achieved by slow, careful drawing of outlines and shapes and subtle shading.

EUGENE DELACROIX (1798–1863)

The great Romantic French painter Delacroix could draw brilliantly. He believed that his work should show the essential characteristics of the subject matter he was portraying. This meant that the elemental power and vigour of the scene, people or objects should be transmitted to the viewer in the most immediate way possible. His vigorous, lively drawings are more concerned with capturing life than including minuscule details for the sake of it. He would only include as much detail as was necessary to convince the viewer of the verisimilitude of his subject. As you can see from these examples, his loose powerful lines pulsate with life.

JOSEPH MALLORD WILLIAM TURNER (1775–1851)

Turner started his career as a topographical painter and draughtsman and made his living producing precise and recognizable drawings of places of interest. He learnt to draw everything in the landscape, including all the information that gives the onlooker back the memory of the place he has seen. This ability stayed with him, even after he began to paint looser and more imaginative and elemental landscapes. Although the detail is not so evident in these canvases, which the Impressionists considered the source of their investigations into the breaking up of the surface of the picture, the underlying knowledge of place and appearance remains and contributes to their great power.

The outline drawing of the abbey (shown left) is an early piece, and amply illustrates the topographic exactitude for which the artist was famous in his early years. The second example is much more a painter's sketch, offering large areas of tone and flowing lines to suggest the effect of a coastal landscape.

EDGAR DEGAS (1834–1917)

Degas was taught by a pupil of Ingres, and studied drawing in Italy and France until he was the most expert draughtsman of all the Impressionists. His loose flowing lines, often repeated several times to get the exact feel, look simple but are inordinately difficult to master. The skill evident in his paintings and drawings came out of continuous practice. He declared that his epitaph should be: 'He greatly loved drawing'. He would often trace and retrace his own drawings in order to get the movement and grace he was after. Hard work and constant efforts to improve his methods honed his natural talent.

PIERRE AUGUSTE RENOIR (1841–1919)

Renoir could be called the man who loved women. His pictures of young women, dressed or undressed, are some of the sweetest drawings of the female form ever produced. He always has the painter's eye and sacrifices any detail to the main effect of the picture. When he does produce a detail, it is extremely telling and sets the tone for the rest of the picture. His drawings and paintings of late 19th century Paris are imbued with an extremely happy atmosphere which has captured the imagination of artists ever since.

GEORGES SEURAT (1859–91)

Seurat's style of drawing is very different from what we have seen so far; mainly because he was so interested in producing a mass or area of shape that he reduced many of his drawings to tone alone. In these pictures there are no real lines but large areas of graduated tone rendered in charcoal, conté or thick pencil on faintly grainy textured paper. Their beauty is that they convey both substance and atmosphere while leaving a lot to the viewer's imagination. The careful grading of tone is instructive, as is how one mass can be made to work against a lighter area.

PAUL CÉZANNE (1839–1906)
Cézanne attempted to produce drawings and paintings that were true to the reality of form as he saw it. He is the structural master-draughtsman without parallel in this section. All artists since his time owe him a debt of gratitude. His great contribution to art was to produce a body of work that saw the world from more than one viewpoint. The Cubists were inspired by his example to try to draw the objective world from many angles – whether or not they succeeded is arguable.

HENRI MATISSE (1869–1954)

Even without the aid of bright, rich colours Matisse could invest his work with great sensuality. His drawings are marvellously understated yet graphic thanks to the fluidity of line. Awkwardness is evident in some of them, but even with these you never doubt that they express exactly what he wanted. There are no extraneous marks to diffuse the image and confuse the eye. As he got older and suffered from arthritis in his hands, Matisse resorted to drawing with charcoal on the end of a long stick. Despite this handicap, the large, simple images he produced by this method possess great power.

PABLO PICASSO (1881–1973)

Picasso dominated the art world for the greater part of the 20th century. He took every type of artistic tradition and reinvented it, demonstrating that a master-artist can break all the rules and still produce work that strikes a chord with the casual observer. The image below, for example, is an interesting hybrid among the other examples shown here: two pieces of toned paper cut out for the neck and face with the features and hair drawn in with pencil.

Although he distorted conventional shapes almost out of recognition, the final result was imbued with the essence of the subject he was illustrating. He experimented in all mediums, but in his drawings we can see the amazing dexterity with which he confounded our preconceptions and gave us a new way of seeing art. His sketchbooks reveal his wide range of abilities and are an inspiration to all artists.

HENRY CARR (1894–1970)
The English illustrator and painter Henry Carr was an excellent draughtsman, as these portraits show. He produced some of the most attractive portraits of his time because of his ability to adapt his medium and style to the qualities of the person he was drawing. The subtlety of the marks he makes to arrive at his final drawing varies, but the result is always sensitive and expressive. A noted teacher, his book on portraiture is well worth studying.

The Experience of Drawing

As you have learnt from the previous section, there is no substitute for observation in drawing. When you look long and hard at anything that you wish to draw, ask yourself the question, 'What am I seeing?' Don't just give yourself answers like 'a landscape', 'a teapot', 'a human being', etc, because such answers close down your observation. Look instead at colour, shape, form, texture, outline and movement. These apply to everything visual and help you to analyse your impressions, which can assist your seeing. However, keep looking, even when you think you know what you're looking at. Nothing stays the same for more than a few seconds; the light changes, for example, giving you a new version of what you're looking at, even if it's only a still form. The exciting thing about all this is that you never get bored. There is infinite variety, even in familiar scenes that we see every day.

When you start to draw from life it is always difficult to see how to make the three-dimensional image in front of you fit onto the paper without it looking awkward, stiff, inaccurate or flat. There is no avoiding this exercise, however, if you want to find out whether you have real drawing ability.

In this section we'll be looking at a range of subjects as they really are: agglomerations of shapes. As well as the shapes of the things themselves, you will notice the shapes between things. There are no spaces in drawing or painting, just other areas of tone. You will find with the subjects you choose that the shapes butt up tightly to one another. Look at the whole image with interest and without preconception. Try to notice everything and don't regard one part of the whole as superior to the rest. It is not.

ANALYZING SHAPES

Ordinarily when you look at a scene, object or person, your eyes will first register the shapes in an objective way and then your mind will supply information that enables you to recognize what you are seeing. The names, concepts or labels the mind supplies are not helpful to you as an artist, however, and you need to ignore them if you are to see objectively the shapes that are actually there.

One way of getting a more objective view is to analyse the shapes you are looking at in terms of their geometry. For example, a circular object seen at any angle forms an ellipse, and if you know how to draw an ellipse correctly you will get a good image of the object. Anything spherical is just a circle with toning to fool the eye into believing in the object's sphericality.

The spaces between objects are often triangles or rectangles. Objects within a group can be seen as being at different angles to each other: a leg may be propped up at an angle of 45 degrees from the upright torso, and the lower leg may be at right-angles to the thigh.

This sort of visual analysis is very useful for you, the observer, to undertake and will help the accuracy of your drawing. Once you recognize the angles you are drawing, you will find it difficult to draw them badly.

Observing a subject in almost geometric terms helps to simplify our approach to drawing. Look at this very simple picture. Both figures can be contained in a triangle. To the right of the little girl the space can be cut off along her right side so that she and her father's legs fit into a parallelogram. The space under her left arm, extending to her father's foot, makes another triangle.

Measuring Proportions

Another useful form of analysis is to employ some common unit of measurement to get the proportions of different objects in your drawing right. For example, the shape and size of a door or window can give you a basic unit of measurement with which to measure the other units in a composition. In figure drawing, the head is a useful unit for measuring the human body. If you use a form of analysis, just remember that the unit has to remain constant throughout the composition, otherwise the proportion will not be right.

Rule of thumb is one of the most common units of measurement (see opposite page). The logic of this method is that your arm will not grow any longer during the time it takes to complete your drawing, so no matter how many measurements you take, your measuring device will remain at the same distance from your eye. Remember, though, that if you move your position you will have to start again because every proportion may alter.

Using rule of thumb

Here the rule of thumb measurement is used to gauge the proportions of a figure. The arm is outstretched and the pencil held upright in line with the drawing board. The measurement taken (of the head, in this instance) is called 'sight-size'.

Once the measurement is taken it can be transferred to the paper. As long as you measure everything in your scene in this way, staying the same distance from the model and

keeping the pencil at arm's length when measuring, the method will give you a fairly accurate range of proportions.

This method is of limited value to beginners, however: the drawing will not be large and beginners really need to draw large in order to correct their mistakes more easily. Experienced artists will be able to translate the proportions into larger measurements when drawing larger than sight-size.

TECHNICAL AIDS

Photographs and slides can be used by artists to render a scene accurately. What they can not give is a personal and thus richer view of a subject. This can only be achieved if the artist takes the time to go to the actual scene and look for himself.

The old masters used tools such as the *camera obscura* and *camera lucida* – literally, 'dark room' and 'light room' – to ensure the accuracy of their perspective and proportion. Another device used by artists of old to help this sort of technical analysis was a draughtsman's net or grid. This was a screen with crossed strings or wires creating a net or grid of exactly measured squares through which the artist could look at a scene. As long as the artist ensured that his eye was always in the same position each time he looked through the screen, and as long as a similar grid was drawn on his sheet of paper, the main composition could be laid out and each part related correctly.

These methods are not ends in themselves, however, and although they provide the main outlines of a composition, they cannot give the subtle distinctions that make a work of art attractive. To capture these, the artist has to use his own eye and judgement.

The draughtsman's net or grid is a construct for use in the Renaissance manner. Usually artists make them themselves or have them made by a framemaker. The squares can be either marked directly onto the glass or indicated by stretching thin cords or wires across a frame. The glass is then set in a stand through which the object is viewed.

Patience is required to transfer the image of a subject viewed in this way onto paper: it is very easy to keep moving your head and thus changing your view in relation to both the frame and the subject. The trick is to make sure that the mark on the object and the mark on the grid where two lines meet are correctly aligned each time you look.

Canaletto and Vermeer are just two of the artists who used the *camera obscura* in their work. It has the same effect as the *camera lucida*, although achieving it by different means. Used by painters for landscapes, cityscapes and interior scenes, the device was a tent or small room with a pin-hole or lens in one side which cast an image of the object onto a glass screen or sheet of paper, which could then be traced. It was an excellent device for architectural forms as long as one ignored the outer limits of the image, which tended to be distorted.

In a camera lucida or lucidograph a prism is used to transfer the image of a scene onto paper or board. This enables the artist to draw around the basic shape to get the proportions correct before he looks normally at the object.

The technique was well adapted for use in small areas of drawing and was probably favoured by illustrators and painters for portraits or still lifes. The lucidograph was used extensively by Ingres and possibly Chardin and Fantin Latour; David Hockney was encouraged to try it in his work after he detected the method in the drawings of Ingres.

A slide-projector can give a similar effect to a lucidograph, although of course it allows you to use a much larger format and any kind of scene that can be photographed. It has been used extensively by artists who want to reproduce master paintings or enlarge their own work. Its only drawback is the difficulty of keeping your shadow out of the way.

PROPORTIONS IN DETAIL

It is easy enough after some practice to remember the basic proportions of the human face seen from the front and the human body seen standing erect in full view. You will find other subjects much more variable, however. For them you will need to use a system to help you ensure that the different parts of your composition are in proportion to each other. This is particularly true when there is a lot of perspective depth in a scene, requiring you to show the relationship between the objects closer to you and the objects further away. Even in landscapes, where a certain amount of cheating (politely called 'artistic licence') is allowable because of the tremendous variation in proportions depending on your viewpoint, it is necessary to have some method of organizing the proportions of trees to houses to people and to far-away objects on the horizon. Even more important than ordering these variables is an accurate assessment of the angle of objects to your eye-level.

When the eye-level is low, smaller, closer objects dominate the view much more than when the eye-level is high. Trees on the skyline can look bigger or nearer when they are silhouetted against the light, because they have more definition. If there is a large object in the centre of your composition, it will tend to grab the eye. There is even a proportional effect in colour and tone. A very bright or very dark object standing in sharp contrast to the background grabs the attention, and even if this object is quite small it will appear larger than it is. The effect is that quite small objects of strong tone or colour will give an appearance of being larger than they are.

A well-defined dark silhouette on the skyline set against a light sky will dominate a scene and appear closer than it really is.

A bright, light object standing out against a dark-toned background will dominate a scene despite its small size.

FORESHORTENING

When drawing objects or people seen from one end and looking along the length of the object or figure, the parts of the object nearer to your eye will appear much larger when compared to those at the further end. Many beginners find this truth quite difficult to grasp. The belief that the head cannot possibly be as large as the legs tends to influence them into disregarding the evidence of their own eyes and amending their drawing to fit their misconception. However, it is easy enough to make a simple measurement to help convince the mind of what the eye actually sees. Try it for yourself after you have studied the next drawing.

The strange proportions of foreshortening

Note the depth of the head (4 ½ units), which is the same as the open hand, and the foreshortened forearm and foreshortened leg. At 8 units the torso is only just less than twice the size of the head. The full length of
the body from shoulder to ankle (10 ½ units) is just over twice the head. The upper arm is the same length as the torso (8 units). The distance from elbow to elbow (23) is longer than the distance from head to heel (15).

THE EFFECT OF DIFFERENT EYE-LEVELS

These three drawings show how the effect of a picture is altered by the relationship of figures to the horizon or eye-line. In the first two pictures the viewer is standing and in the last picture the viewer is seated. This change in the relationship of the figures to the horizon-line has had quite an effect on the composition, and has indeed changed its dynamic.

You can see in galleries of paintings how artists have used this dynamic, particularly the Impressionists – look at examples of the work of Degas and Monet.

In the first picture the eye-level is considerably higher than the people reclining on the beach. The viewer has a sense of looking down on the figures, which appear to be part of the overall scene and are not at all dominant.

The eye-level of these two standing figures is the same as ours, making them appear more active. We are standing, as are they. (Note that the line of the horizon is at the same level as their eyes.)

Here the eye-level is much lower than that of the two figures; even the girl bending down is still head and shoulders above our eye-level. The figures now appear much more important and powerful in the composition.

ODD PROPORTIONS

The importance of relating proportions within the human figure correctly becomes very apparent when you have a figure in which some parts are foreshortened and others are not. In this example you'll notice that the right leg and arm are pointing towards the viewer, whereas the left leg and arm are not. As a result, the area taken up by the respective legs and arms is quite different in both proportion and shape. The right arm is practically all hand and shoulder and doesn't have the length evident with the left arm. The right leg is almost a square shape and strikingly different from the long rectangles of the left leg. The rectangles about the head and torso are also interestingly compared with the different arms and legs.

Once you begin to see such proportional differences within a subject, you will find your drawing of the whole becomes easier.

VIVE LA DIFFERENCE

People are not alike in form, and few conform to the classical ideal. The examples shown here are of the same height and vertical proportion but vastly different in width. If presented to the inexperienced artist in a life class, both would be problematical, because beginners tend to draw what they think people should look like, and will even out oddities to fit their preconceptions. Often they will slim down a fat model or fatten up a thin one. If they themselves are slim, they will draw the model slimmer than they are. Conversely, if they are on the solid side, they will add flesh to the model. In effect they are drawing what they know, not what they see. This doesn't result in accurate draughtsmanship and has to be eliminated if progress is to be made. Remember: horizontal proportions are measured in exactly the same way as vertical proportions.

AREAS OF DARK AND LIGHT
In all three drawings shown here notice how the light areas outline the dark shapes and dark areas outline the light shapes. You will find that some shapes run into each other to make a large shape and this is often easier to draw than a multitude of smaller shapes.

Very large geometric shapes, such as walls, doors and windows, (left and opposite page) can provide a natural grid for a picture, making it easier to place other shapes, such as figures or, in an outdoor scene, trees.

In this drawing, based on a Vermeer, the simplified forms of the figures show clearly against the large expanse of the wall and floor. The framed picture helps to place the figures, as does the table and chair. The window, the source of light, is very dominant against the dark wall.

ANGLES

Look at the angles in the figure shown below. As long as you can visualize a right-angle (90 degrees) and half a right-angle (45 degrees), and possibly a third (30 degrees) or two-thirds (60 degrees) of a right-angle, you should have no difficulty making sense of them. Let's break them down:

The wall in relation to the horizontal base on which the figure is resting is a right-angle (90 degrees) (A). But what about the rest of the angles shown?

(B) – the angle of the torso to the horizontal base.
(C) – the angle between the thigh and the horizontal base.
(D) – the angle between the thigh and the lower leg.
(E) – the angle between the lower leg and the horizontal base.
(F) – the angle of the head to the torso.
(G) – the angle of the head to the wall.

All these questions need to be answered. Just ask yourself – is it a full right-angle, or just less, or just more? Is it nearer a third or nearer a half right-angle? Accurate answers to these questions will help you to envisage the structure of the drawing on the page correctly.

ANSWERS:
B. A bit more than 45 degrees, perhaps 60.
C. About 45 degrees.
D. A bit less than 90 degrees (almost a right-angle).
E. About 45 degrees.
F. About 120 degrees (one right-angle plus a third).
G. A bit less than 30 degrees.

RELATING TRIANGLES AND RECTANGLES

The lines in the next drawing may look complex but they are in fact a way of simplifying a grouping by pinpointing the extremities of the figures. Adopting this method will also help you to hold the composition in your mind while you are drawing.

Let's identify the triangular relationships in this fairly natural composition: the father's head to his lower foot and to the mother's lower foot; also his head to his hands; the boy's head with his feet; the father's knees and feet; the mother's skirt shape and the relationship of head to elbow to knee. The table and lamp form a ready-made triangle.*

Triangles and Angles Simplified

You don't have to be a great geometrician to understand systems based on angles and triangles. When it comes to triangles, just note the relative sizes of their sides: in an equilateral triangle all three sides are equal (and all angles are equal); in an isoceles triangle one side is shorter than the other two; and in a parallelogram the opposite sides are equal in length and parallel.

Angles are even simpler. An angle of 90 degrees looks like the corner of a square. Half a right-angle is 45 degrees, and a third is 30 degrees. These are the only angles you'll need to be able to recognize. All the others can be related to them, and thought of in terms of more or less than 30, 45 or 90 degrees.

HUMAN ARCHITECTURE

Learning to relate the skeleton and muscular structure of the body to the outer appearance becomes more important as you progress with figure drawing. You will need to study the structure of the body in detail if you really want your drawings to look convincing. The drawing below gives you some idea of the complexity of detail involved.

    The Renaissance artists, of course, learnt about anatomy from dissected human and animal bodies. However, for most of us books on anatomy are quite good enough to give the main shapes, although a real skeleton (which quite a few artists and doctors have) will give more detailed information.

Splenius copitis

Rhomboidius major and minor

Trapezius

Deltoid

Triceps

Latissimus dorsi

Obliquus externus abdominis

Gluteus medius

Gluteus maximus

THE HEAD

The head is defined mostly by the shape of the skull underneath its thin layer of muscle, and to a lesser extent by the eye-balls. The rather flat groups of muscles on the skull produce all our facial expressions, so it is very useful to have some idea of their arrangement and function, especially if you want to draw portraits.

Muscles of the Head

A. *Corrugator (pulls eyebrows together)*

B. *Frontalis (moves forehead and eyebrows)*

C. *Temporalis (helps move jaw upwards)*

D. *Orbicularis oculis (closes eye)*

E. *Compressor nasi (narrows nostrils, pushes nose down)*

F. *Quadratus labii superioris (raises upper lip)*

G. *Zygomaticus major (upward traction of mouth)*

H. *Levator anguli oris (raises angle of mouth)*

I. *Orbicularis oris (closes mouth, purses lips)*

J. *Masseter (upward traction of lower jaw)*

K. *Buccinator (lateral action of mouth, expels fluid or air from cheeks)*

L. *Risorius (lateral pulling on angle of mouth)*

M. *Depressor anguli oris (downward traction of angle of mouth)*

N. *Depressor labii inferioris (downward pulling of lower lip)*

O. *Mentalis (moves skin on chin)*

Bones of the Skull

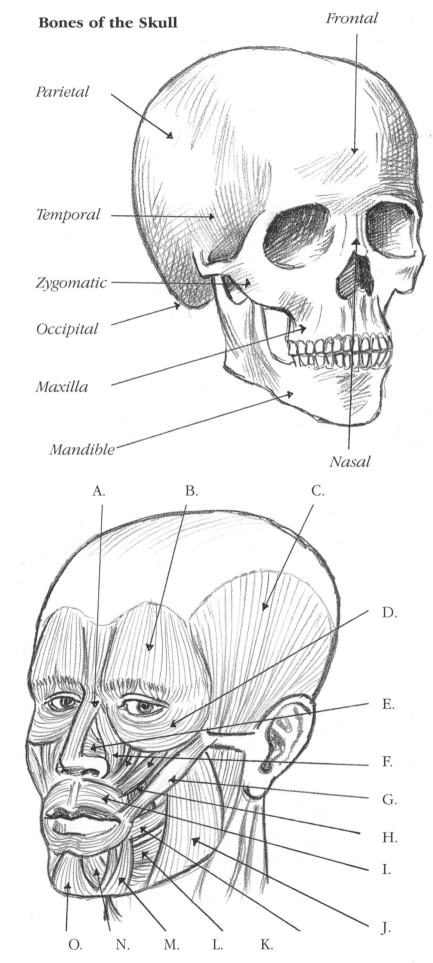

Frontal

Parietal

Temporal

Zygomatic

Occipital

Maxilla

Mandible

Nasal

A. B. C.

D.

E.

F.

G.

H.

I.

J.

O. N. M. L. K.

ELLIPSES

An ellipse is a circle seen from an oblique angle. Ellipses on the same level above or below the eye level will be similar in proportion. Several circular objects on a circular base will have the same proportions, as you will see if you look at the drawing below.

The lampshade, base of the lamp-stand, table-top, and top and bottom of the glass are all ellipses related to the same eye-level. The lower ellipses are related to the same eye level and as they are all about the same level they will be very similar in proportions of width to height although of different sizes.

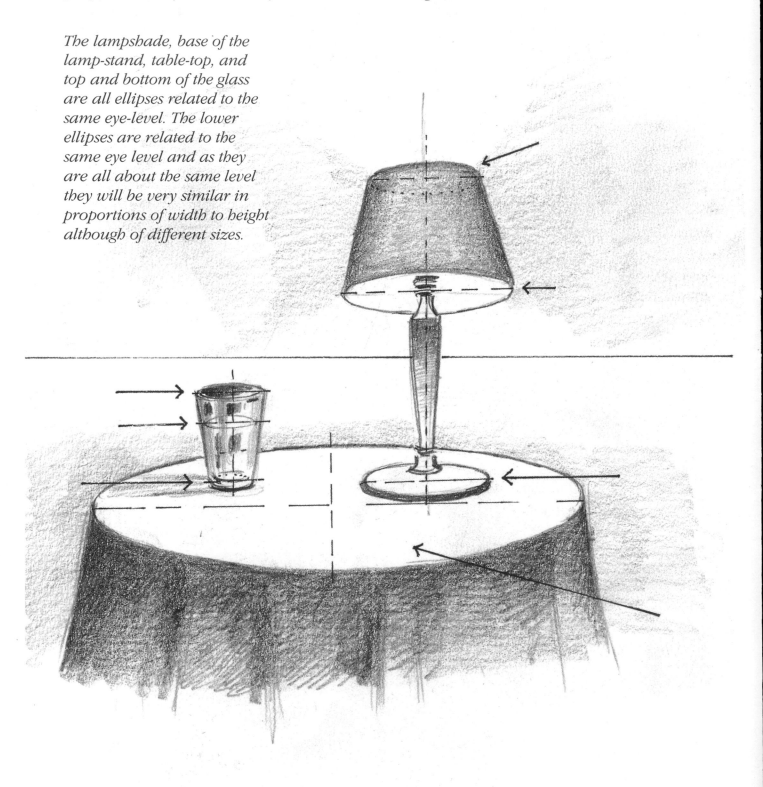

USING A COMMON UNIT OF MEASUREMENT

A large subject such as a street scene, in which proportions and perspective have to be taken into account, can be difficult to draw accurately unless you use some system of measurement.

For the urban scene shown below, I chose an element within the scene as my unit of measurement (the lower shuttered window facing out of the drawing) and used it to check the proportions of each area in the composition. As you can see, the tall part of the building facing us is about six times the height of the shuttered window. The width of the whole building is twice the height of the shuttered window in its taller part and additionally six times the height of the shuttered window in its lower, one-storey part near the edge of the picture.

6 units

just over 2 units

2 units

1 unit

1 unit

Just over 1 unit

2 units

6 units

Keeping Measurement in Perspective

A unit of measurement enables us to maintain the accuracy of our drawing, but it is only meant to provide a rough guide. Once you are used to drawing you will find the eye an extraordinarily accurate instrument for judging proportion and size. Sometimes we just need to check to make sure we've got them right, and at such times units and the like come into their own.

PERSPECTIVE

There are many things to be borne in mind with perspective. The main point is that it is impossible to put down exactly what we see in the two dimensions of drawing and painting. A certain amount of adjustment and artistic licence has to be allowed. A flat map can't replicate the world's surface, which is curved, and so will have to sacrifice either area shape or area proportion. When we look at something ordinarily, our eyes scan the scene. However, when we look at a picture, our vision is drawn as though from one point. This means that the outside edges of the cone of vision (as it's called) will not be easily drawn with any accurate relationship to the centre of vision. The artist, therefore, has to limit his area of vision to one that can be taken in at one glance. The artist must also be aware of his own eye-level or where the horizon really is, however much it is obscured by hills, trees or buildings. The actual cone or field of vision is about 60 degrees, but the artist will limit his picture to much less unless he is going to show distortion.

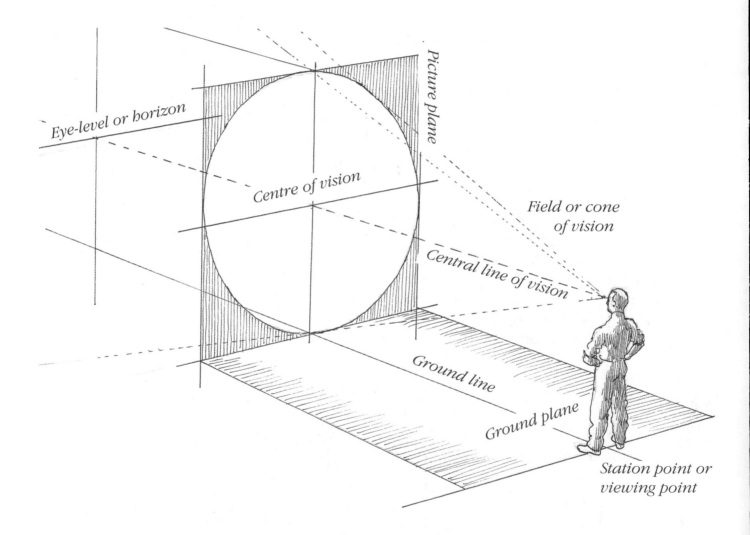

RELATIONSHIPS IN THE PICTURE PLANE

In the example shown here we look at the relationships between the tree, post and flowers and the horizon line. As you can see, the height of the tree in the picture appears not as high as the post, although in reality the post is smaller than the tree. This is due to the effect of perspective, the tree being further away than the post. There is also an area of ground between the bottom of the tree and the flower. The horizon line is the same as the eye-level of the viewer.

Post and top of tree will appear level.

The height of the tree in relation to the post.

Area of ground seen between base of tree and flower.

Distant horizon or eye-level of viewer.

Distance between bottom of tree and bottom of post.

AERIAL PERSPECTIVE

When you are drawing scenes that include a distant landscape as well as close up elements, you must give the eye an idea of how much air or space there is between the foreground, middle ground and background. In this drawing these areas are clearly delineated. The buildings and lamp-posts close to the viewer are sharply defined and have texture and many tonal qualities. The buildings further away are less defined, with fewer tonal variations. The cliffs behind this built-up area are very faint, with no detail or texture and without much variation in tone.

PERSPECTIVE: ALBERTI'S SYSTEM

The Renaissance architect and scholar Leon Battista Alberti (1404–72) put together a system of producing perspective methods for artists based on Filippo Brunelleschi's (1377–1446) discoveries in the science of optics. His system enabled a new generation of painters, sculptors and architects to visualize the three dimensions of space and use them in their work.

With Alberti's system the artist has to produce a ground plan of rectangles in perspective and then build structures onto this base. In order to do this he has to work out a way of drawing up the plan relating to the rays of vision and the eye-level or horizon so that measured divisions on the plan can be transferred into an apparent open window onto the scene being depicted. The viewpoint of artist and viewer is central and on the eye-level line, and this gives the picture conviction in depth and dimension.

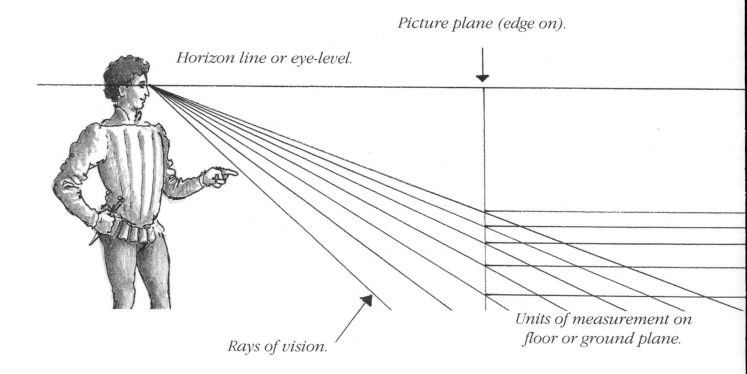

Picture plane (edge on).

Horizon line or eye-level.

Rays of vision.

Units of measurement on floor or ground plane.

Using Alberti's ground plan

Once you have produced the ground plan grid, with the eye-level and vanishing point, you can then decide the height of your object or building – in the example shown right, it is 5 units of the floor grid. Using a compass, describe two arcs to connect verticals drawn from the four corners of the proposed building to the edges of the top of the

structure; draw horizontal lines for the near and far edges, and lines connected to the vanishing point for the two side edges.

The projections of front and side elevations shown here give a very simple structure. Alberti's system can be used to determine the look of far more complex structures than the one illustrated.

Producing Alberti's ground plan

The ground line is measured in units that are related to a vanishing point on the horizon and can be seen as related to the picture plane. A simple diagonal drawn across the resulting chequered pavement can be used to check the accuracy of the device.

Once the pavement effect has been produced, any other constructions can be placed in the space, convincing the viewer

that he is looking into a three-dimensional space. This only works because of the assumptions we make about size and distance. If the lines of perspective are disguised to look like real things, such as pavements and walls, the eye accepts the convention and 'sees' an image understood as depth in the picture. Of course, all details have to conform in order to convince.

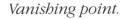

Vanishing point.

Checking line (to check the integrity of the grid).

Transversals (horizontal lines connecting rays of vision from picture plane to perspective construction).

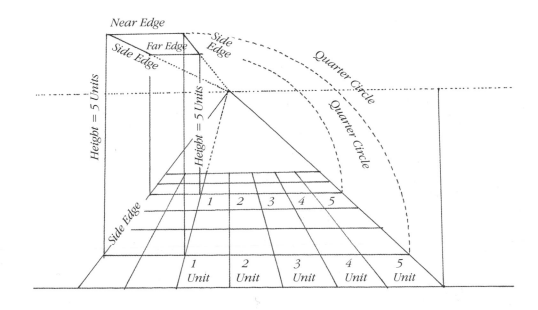

Near Edge
Far Edge
Side Edge
Side Edge
Side Edge
Side Edge
Quarter Circle
Quarter Circle
Height = 5 Units
Height = 5 Units

1   2   3   4   5

1 Unit   2 Unit   3 Unit   4 Unit   5 Unit

PERSPECTIVE: FIELD OF VISION

The system we look at next is quite easy to construct. You don't require training in mathematics to get it right, just the ability to use a ruler, set square and compass precisely. Although the picture does not have depth in actuality, the eye is satisfied that it does, because it sees an area of squares which reduces geometrically as it recedes into the background.

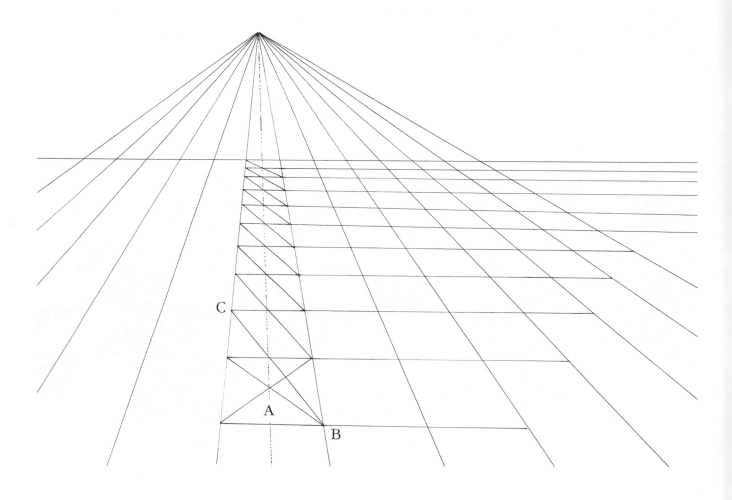

Constructing an area of squares

Any square portions, such as paving slabs, tiles or even a chequer-board of fields, can be used to prove the illusion of depth in a picture.

Take one slab or square size (A), draw in diagonal lines and from the crossing point of these diagonals mark a construction line to the vanishing point. In order to get the next rows of paving slabs related to the first correctly and in perspective, draw a line from the near corner (B) to the point where the construction line to the vanishing point

cuts the far edge of the square. Continue it until it cuts the next line to the vanishing point (C) and then construct your next horizontal edge to the next paving slab. Repeat in each square until you reach the point where the slabs should stop in the distance. Having produced a row of diminishing slabs, you can continue the horizontal edges of the slabs in either direction to produce the chequer-board of the floor. Notice the impressive effect you get when you fill in alternate squares.

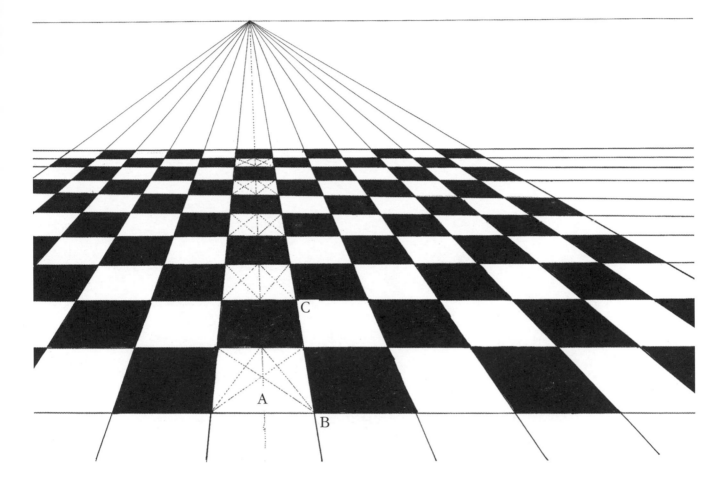

More About Chequer-Board

The sort of chequer-board floor or pavement you have been learning about has often been used in paintings to help the illusion of depth. In early Renaissance pictures it was thought to be amazingly realistic. These days we are a bit more used to seeing such devices and so other effects have been brought into play to help us accept the illusion of dimensionality. However, do experiment with the chequer-board ground – it's very simple and very effective. And don't forget to incorporate the lessons you've learnt about the relationship of figure to the horizon or eye-line: if you place figures or objects on it, make sure that as they recede into the picture – standing on squares that are further back – they diminish in size consistent with your eye level (see pages 54–55).

MOVEMENT

Drawing movement is not as difficult as it might seem at first, although it does need quite a lot of practice. You'll find it helpful if you can feel the movement you are portraying in your own body, because this will inform the movement you are trying to draw. The more you know about movement the better. It's a good idea to observe people's movements to check out how each part of the anatomy behaves in a range of poses and attitudes.

Photographs of bodies in action are very useful, but limited in the range they offer. It is noticeable that action shots tend to capture moments of impact or of greatest force. Rarely do you find an action shot of the movements in-between. With a bit of careful observation, watching and analyzing, you should be able to see how to fill in the positions between the extremes.

Here we see a man in the various stages of throwing a javelin. The point at which he is poised to throw and the moment when the javelin is launched are the two extremes of this process. However, you may find that drawing the man in a position between these extremes gives you a composition with more drama and tension.

Similarly here, the point between the head completing its turn from one side to the other offers a different quality and perhaps a more revealing perspective on the subject.

In these examples the only really obvious movement is the hand lifting the cup to drink. The first drawing sets the scene; the second shows the intent; and the third completes the action. The loose multiple line used in the second and third drawings helps to give the effect of movement.

MOVEMENT: CONTROLLED AND UNCONTROLLED

The most effective drawings of people falling accidentally capture the sheer unpredictability of the situation. In this example the arms and legs are at all sorts of odd angles and the expression is a mixture of tension, fear and surprise. He is wondering where and how he's going to land. Deliberately I made the line rather uncertain to enhance the effect of the uncertainty in the situation.

In this example, the odd angle of the viewer's vision provides a contrast with the lines of the water and side of the pool, creating tension although it's obvious what is happening. This is not drama in the making but a moment frozen in time. The slight strobe effect of the diving-board also helps to give the impression that we are witnessing something first-hand.

I used a clip from a newspaper as my model for this rugby player kicking a ball. My version is slightly amended from the original to accentuate the 'fuzz' of the out-of-focus kicking foot. The speed of this movement contrasts with the rest of the figure, which is much more clearly defined. The balance of the position is very important, to accentuate the force of the kick and the concentration of the kicker on those distant goal-posts.

ADDING TO YOUR VOCABULARY

A practising artist must be ready to draw at any time. If you want to excel at drawing, sketching has to become a discipline. Get into the habit of seeing things with a view to drawing them. This means, of course, that you'll have to carry a sketch-pad around with you, or something that you can jot your impressions in. You'll find yourself making sketches of unrepeatable one-offs that can't be posed, as I did with some of the sketches shown here.

A quick note, even if not very accurate, is all you need to make a worthwhile addition to your vocabulary of drawing. Often it is impossible to finish the sketch, but this doesn't matter. Some of the most evocative drawings any artist produces are quick, spontaneous sketches that capture the fleeting movement, attitude, angle of vision or view of a movement. They are often the drawings you return to again and again to use in compositions or to remind yourself of an atmosphere or place.

When drawing scenes with large areas of building it is useful to simplify the areas of light and shade to make it more obvious how the light defines the solidity of the buildings. In both these examples a large area of shadow anchors the whole composition and gives it depth and strength.

In the first drawing we are aware that the open area with buildings around it is a square; in the second we are in no doubt that the very dark area is an arch through a solid building. In both examples the light and shade help to convince.

Don't Forget Your Sketch-Book

A pocket-sized book with hard covers and thinnish paper is generally the best for most quick sketches, being simple to use and forcing you to be economic with your lines, tones or colours. A clutch pencil or lightweight plastic propelling pencil with a fine lead is ideal; preferably carry more than one. A fine line pigment liner is also very useful and teaches you to draw with confidence no matter how clumsy the drawing.

Continual practice makes an enormous difference to your drawing skill and helps you to experiment in ways to get effects down fast and effectively. If you're really serious you should have half a dozen sketch-books of varying sizes and papers, but hard-backed ones are usually easier to use because they incorporate their own built-in drawing board. A large A2 or A3 sketch-book can be easily supported on the knees when sitting and give plenty of space to draw. Cover the pages with many drawings, rather than having one on each page, unless your drawing is so big that it leaves no room for others.

Form and Shape

What the eye sees is shape, colour, light and shade, and not much else. However, the mind goes to work on the experience, relates it to other experiences and translates the shape and form into something we can recognize, such as a man, woman, horse, dog, tree, house or whatever.

Shape is the outline visual impression we have of an object. However, because we get used to seeing certain objects in certain positions our minds develop visual templates and we tend to see what we expect to see rather than what is actually there. Shape changes constantly, depending on our position in relation to it, and this can cause us endless problems as viewers and artists.

Form is the three-dimensional appearance of an object or body; in other words, the spatial area it inhabits. Form is more difficult to draw than shape because of the problems of representing three dimensions on a flat surface. To make our representations realistic, we have to find ways of expressing shapes coming towards the viewer or receding from the viewpoint.

The artist has to experiment both in seeing and drawing in order to come to an understanding of the language of shape and form and how to manipulate it. This section is intended to help you use your eyes more experimentally, to look beyond your expectations and your normal process of recognition.

ARCHITECTURAL FORMS

To understand form in space we need to exercise our spatial awareness, and not simply analyse by what we would expect to see as shaped by what we know from theory. When it comes to architecture, which surrounds most of us most of the time, we need to start looking at it with our spatial and visual senses honed to a more perceptive state.

When we look at the shape of an example of Gothic vaulting, or an example of Islamic vaulting, we see that there is a need for, and therefore a certain similarity in, the techniques used to over-arch a space. But the way these architectural forms have been specifically designed means that they could never be mistaken for each other, even though they both serve the same functional purpose.

This exercising of the visual sense is very important for the artist, so when looking at different forms of architecture, try to forget about what you know, and rely much more on visual stimulus to compare one form with another. Apart from your aesthetic appreciation, it will make drawing architecture much easier.

Gothic (above) and Islamic (left) vaulting share some similarities in terms of the shapes used in their creation, but you could not mistake one type for the other. Look at these two examples, noting their similarities and differences.

Although form tends to follow function, this does not mean it is strait-jacketed by the relationship. Many variations are possible, and this is where choice comes into play. We compare images by being aware of the implications of a form. Our decision to use a form in a picture is based on an assessment of suitability.

Aesthetic and social requirements for living change over time and these can bring about great differences in 'look'. The medieval home (above) was functional for its time, but does not share the sharp, clean-cut lines of its modern counterpart.

SHAPE RECOGNITION
Let's look at a few shapes in silhouette. What clues to identity are carried in these simple outlines?
The American Mustang, the British Spitfire and the German Stuka are all World War Two low-wing
monoplane fighter aircraft. They are easy to tell apart and to identify because of the particular
details evident in their main frames. Similarly, the Harrier jump-jet and Sea King helicopter shown
on the facing page are not difficult to differentiate from other types of aircraft.

Spitfire

*All three of these
fighter aircraft were
produced about the
same time. Each
was intended to be
the best of its type.
The Mustang was
the most effective.*

Mustang

Stuka

Harrier

*Both of these types of
aircaft take off vertically
but possess different
means of achieving it.*

Sea King

Our ability to recognize shapes is learned in childhood as we become aware of the wider world. Our visual vocabulary grows according to the means at our disposal. All the silhouettes on this spread arouse memories of my childhood, and the hours I spent poring over them in my picture books.

If we are to draw well, we must have the ability to connect shapes and yet differentiate between them. If we are unable to do this, we will end up producing drawings that have as much character as the images on street signs.

The continent of Africa as seen from a spacecraft. This is so familiar to us from maps that one is surprised by the accuracy of those early map-makers, who did not have the benefit of cameras or spacecraft and yet gave us the correct shape.

A World War Two German Army helmet.

The characteristic shape of a 16th-century Spanish Morion helmet.

Both types of helmet provided protection for the head in battle but had rather different weaponry to contend with.

These two ships have similar functions but evolved in different places with slightly different technologies. The shape of each is characteristic, and you would be unlikely to mistake one for the other.

The Santa Maria, Columbus's craft.

A Chinese junk.

SYMBOLS AND ASSOCIATIONS

Some buildings become the signatures of places or legends, because of the association made for them. If we see a picture of the Eiffel Tower, we immediately think 'Paris'. When we see an image of the Taj Mahal, even a sketchy drawing such as the one shown, associations of India or the East come into our minds. Similarly, Cervantes' creation Don Quixote will forever be associated with Spanish windmills.

There are many other examples of images which are indelibly associated with places, things or ideas. How many can you think of?

Instinctive recognition is an odd effect of partly seeing and partly expecting. When you are trying to draw the shape of something, it becomes clear that it has characteristics that help to define its role. Its shape enables it to do what it does.

The shape of the most aggressive predator in the ocean is very well-known to us from our experience of films and photographs. There is no mistaking its formidable shape, even in silhouette. How is it that the outline of a white swan on a dark background is so peaceful, while that black, shark shape is so full of sinister power? Because we know how these shapes affect the viewer and the associations they attach to them.

As artists we can use this knowledge to convey messages in our pictures. This isn't as easy as it sounds if we wish to make our picture work properly. It demands an awareness of shapes and their associations for viewers across broad and disparate areas of life.

Archetypal images of opposites: danger and serenity.

CREATING FORM

Our fairly sophisticated recognition system has to be persuaded to interpret shapes as three-dimensional form. One way of doing this is to produce an effect that will be read as form, although in reality this may only comprise an arrangement of lines and marks. Let's look at some examples.

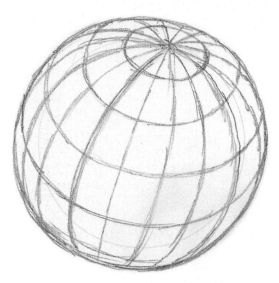

A diagrammatic form is often given in atlases to represent the world. Why is it that this particular arrangement of lines inside a circle makes a fairly convincing version of a sphere with its latitude and longitude lines? We don't really think it is a sphere, but nevertheless it carries conviction as a diagram.

Let's go a stage further. In this drawing of a bleached out photograph of an onion the reduced striations or lines make the same point. We recognize this kind of pattern and realize that what we are looking at is intended to portray a spherical object which sprouts. We can 'see' an onion.

So is this a round fruit? No, of course not. But the drawn effect of light and shade is so familiar from our study of photographs and film that we recognize the rotund shape as a piece of fruit.

Visual Conditioning

We have been educated to accept the representation of three-dimensional objects on a flat surface. This is not the case in all parts of the world. In some remote areas, for example, people cannot recognize three-dimensional objects they are familiar with from photographs.

When we look at this hexagonal divided into parallelograms of light, dark and medium tones, we want to interpret it as a cube or block shape.

These rather scribbled lines and marks can be seen as a leaping cat-like creature and a human form engaged in sporting activity. Of course they are not really those things, but there are enough clues to prompt our ever-ready memory to remind us of forms we have seen. The mind quickly fills in the details even when a form is rudimentary.

APPROACHES TO FORM

So what methods can we use to portray form convincingly so that the onlooker sees a solidity that is in fact merely inferred? Well, on these pages we have the human figure – probably the most subtle, difficult but most satisfying subject for drawing – and some details of the eye. These show different ways of analyzing form. Every artist has to undertake his own investigations of form. They involve methods of looking as well as methods of drawing, and through practising them you educate the eye, hand and mind.

We can draw lines around the sections of a form to give us a sort of computerized vision of the dimensions of the shape – as in this recumbent figure.

Another approach is to delineate the different surfaces by drawing marks that are similar to the facets you get on a wooden sculpture. This gives a very real impression of a solid body occupying space.

In a close-up like this, every detail of the form of the eye is shown. It is a very good exercise to take something as obvious as one of our own features, and view it closely in a mirror. Try this yourself: study the form of your eye and then try to draw its every wrinkle or hair or reflection. Note how the lids appear to curve around the smooth ball of the eye itself and how the eyelashes stick out across the lines of the eyelid and the eye.

This could be the under-drawing of the first picture: the diagrammatic form of the main part of the eye with indications of its curves and edges.

The Italian painter Giorgio Morandi had a particular vision of form that is like no other. His etchings of still-life subjects have a dark solidity about them, as in this example. He achieved this effect by piling on fine lines of cross-hatching which, taken in combination, create very substantial, dramatic darks and lights.

As we have already seen with the diagram of the globe on page 88, lines that are built into a diagram can give us all the visual clues we need to an object's shape. In the natural world these lines are often provided for us. Where they do not occur naturally, artists have invented them to help their exploration of form.

In the self-portrait and the view of the village of Estaque shown on this page, Cézanne has somehow managed to show form in space; that is, give an effect of solidity or depth by his rather sparse shading and markings of the shape. He has not shown the classical shade and light relationship, but he hasn't entirely left them out either.

The economy evident in the drawing below is even more pronounced in this landscape. Large areas of blank space are limited by faint markings showing the main blocks of buildings. A few heavier markings here and there emphasize the shadows or intensity of colour in the scene. This rather minimal way of denoting solid masses in space gives a very strong sense of the space between the *buildings in the foreground and those further away. If you decide to show form in this way, be careful not to put in too many lines or heavier marks. Fewer marks seem to produce greater awareness of form in the viewer.*

In this self-portrait the area of darkest tone helps to give the impression of the important areas of form, especially around the eyes and nose. The large tonal areas down one side of the forehead and beard help to connect the main protuberances of the face with the generally rounded shape of the head. With great economy of drawing, Cézanne is able to convince us that we are seeing a three-dimensional head.

These shells are structured in such a way as to provide their own contour lines, the striations or growth lines indications of their natural evolution. Even without light and shade, the clearly seen lines proceeding around the form of the shell give us a good idea of how the shell is shaped. They offer a useful exercise in understanding shapes.

Cézanne tried to discover the form of objects by drawing multiple lines around their edges. He was trying to give multiple views of his objects, such as you get when you view something from many slightly different angles. In this example his lines suggest that you can actually see round the edges of the objects.

Cubism

The Cubists (artists such as Braque, Picasso, Léger and Ozenfant) took Cézanne's analysis one stage further by attempting to draw objects from contrasting viewpoints – from the side, front, above, below, and so on. In the process they had to fragment their images to be able to show these various approaches in one picture. This led to the typical cuboid sets of images for which they were named. These artists were successful in changing how we look at the world, although their methods are rarely employed now.

The most formidable task confronting any artist is how to draw the three-dimensional human form convincingly in one way or another. There are many ways of doing this. Over the next couple of pages we consider three fairly obvious ones.

The work of Franz Stück is linear in style; the bulk of the form is realized with very few lines, allowing our mind to fill in the empty spaces with the fullness of the flesh.

This example, also a copy of a Stück, is more dramatically drawn. Although the edges are soft there is a powerful fullness of form, with chalky looking tonal marks indicating the roundness of the body.

Otto Greiner's approach to form is essentially that of the classical artist, as this copy shows, with the light and shade carefully and sensitively handled. It's an effective if slow and painstaking method, but well worth mastering.

Notice how some lines on the drawing follow the contours around the form and sometimes go across it.

Lines around the contours.

Lines across the contours.

These copies of two heads by David Hockney show different methods of using tone to show form. As a consequence of the different treatment, the effect he has achieved in each drawing is very marked.

The handling here is comparatively sensitive, elegant and very economical, with just enough form showing to enable the viewer to make sense of the shape.

This self-portrait is a much more rugged affair. The dominant tonal area gives us a very generalized feel of the shape of the head, thereby sacrificing individual characteristics to achieve a more dimensional effect.

Whereas on a face all the surfaces move smoothly into each other, even on the craggiest visage, on a building each surface is distinct from the next. Most buildings are rectilinear, cuboid or cylindical and do not have ambiguous curves. The challenge of making a structure that remains upright and lasts in time means that the edges of its surfaces are more sharply defined and the shapes much simpler than those found in natural form. As a consequence it is much easier to show mass.

Here we have two examples of drawings of buildings in which the aim is to communicate something of the materiality and form of these buildings. The first, of a tower by Christopher Wren, follows the shapes almost as if the artist is constructing the building anew as his pencil describes it.

The approach taken for a famous London landmark, Battersea Power Station, is very different, as befits a great monument to an industrial age.

A very powerful three-dimensional effect has been achieved here by vividly portraying the massive simplicity of the building's design with sharply drawn shadows and large light areas.

This drawing captures the elegant balancing forms of classical architecture as practised by Christopher Wren, with spaces through the form and much articulation of the surfaces to create a lightness in the stone structure as well as visual interest.

97

UNIVERSALS IN FORM

Both Ewan Uglow and Geoffrey Elliott produce figures that represent universals in form. Neither is trying to produce portraits in the accepted way. Uglow's figures cannot be said to represent unique, identifiable persons, and Elliott is obviously more interested in the general forms inhabiting the landscape than trying to reproduce individuals on paper. Both approaches teach us that to draw well you don't have to produce an intimate portrait of the person you are drawing. Good drawing can be purely an expression of aesthetics and an experience of form.

These reclining figures are from Geoffrey Elliott's sketch-book of drawings of people on a beach in Sussex. Like Uglow's figures, they are universal in form, but personal qualities emerge despite the absence of obvious emotional expression or movement.

Euan Uglow's masterly way of producing a figure is extremely accurate but time-consuming; he has been known to spend years on just one painting. Uglow built-up this nude figure from hundreds of painstakingly measured marks on canvas or paper to produce an effect of monumentality. This geometric vigour is also reflected in the carefully placed surfaces of tone and colour, which build to a structured and powerful view of the human form. Inevitably this approach necessitates the sacrifice of some elements of individuality.

EXERCISES IN SIMPLIFYING FORM

An object's real shape can be investigated by drawing it from many different angles. For this exercise, we look at a boot, but it could be any object of your choosing. A model can be used for the same exercise. Try drawing him or her from different viewpoints, sometimes standing, sometimes sitting, etc. You will find this detailed investigation into shape very worthwhile.

Simplification is essential if we are to produce accurate drawings. This goes for anything we choose to represent on paper. Lastly on this page, I have chosen a figure for you to practise.

To begin, select an angle from which the object is clearly identifiable. When you have done this, change its position, and continue changing it until you have seen and drawn the object from many different angles – from above, below, on its side, from the front, the back. Continue until you feel that you know how the shape works.

With a still figure it is a good idea to reduce it to its simplest geometric shapes. For example, if the figure is seated on a chair the arrangement could be seen as a rectangular block with a tall tower-like part projecting above. Alternatively, a person sitting with knees up to their chin and arms around their legs produces a wedge-like shape.

Such simplification can greatly assist the business of getting the proportions and the position of the figure correct. Once you have drawn the simple solid geometrical shape, you can draw into it knowing that this is your ground plan.

ELEMENTAL SHAPES

Elemental shapes are as expressive as they are defining, and offer many difficulties when it comes to drawing them. Whatever you do, don't retreat from the problems thrown up by your attempts. All are resolvable if you put in a bit of effort.

A good way to start is by selecting various symbols of the elements and studying them closely. Let's take them in order of difficulty, starting with earth and water.

Earth can be shown by grains of soil or even a turf. Easier still is to choose a tree as your symbol, one whose branches can easily be seen. Winter is, of course, the best time to get a clear view of the architecture of deciduous varieties, which offer the most interesting shapes.

Water is an even harder form to understand than earth. First, try drawing some still water spilt onto a reflective surface, such as a mirror. Careful, detailed study will be necessary to really reveal its properties. Draw the outline edge of the shape first, look at the tonal qualities and then at the reflection in the water. This is not difficult as long as you draw everything you can see.

Moving water provides an even harder challenge. You will need to spend some time watching it and some time simplifying what you see. Eventually, though, you will begin to see the shapes it makes. Sometimes photographs can help in this respect. Don't be too subtle in your initial attempts.

How do you draw what can't be seen? With air, the most obvious way is through the medium of clouds. Beautiful groups of water vapour hanging in the air, forming loose shapes, can describe air very effectively, especially when you see a whole procession of clouds stretching back to the horizon, as here. Try to draw a similar skyscape.

Fire is a really tricky subject. Start with a candle flame before you tackle the flickering flames of a big blaze. You can use photographs for reference, but unless you look closely at a real fire you won't get the feeling of movement or be aware of the variety of shapes.

The early Japanese and Chinese artists had very good ways of drawing flames.

101

INDIVIDUAL EXPRESSION: PICASSO

It's not just the physical forms in a drawing that can be emphasized by careful manipulation of mark making. Pablo Picasso was a master at communicating the qualities that are not so obvious.

In these drawings copied from his sketchbooks, we see three different ways that marks drawn can both correspond to form and put across more emotional messages than just the form's existence in space. They show how an innovative artist can bend the rules of form to recreate form in a new way.

This formal head with an enigmatic expression has the appearance of an African carved wooden mask. The drawing derives its power from the way Picasso has handled the simple surface shapes. There is no attempt to produce the subtler gradations of form. Both flat and curved surfaces have simple modulations.

Here the outline form is an amazing example of a line doing a lot of work to show movement, emotion and spatial dimension. The particular distortions of the forms convey a feeling of substance in a vivid almost rubbery way. The outline is not formal but wiry and energetic and gives a strong impression of drama and emotion.

*In this drawing the extreme emotional power is
brought out by the clever distortion of the
physical shapes of the head without totally
losing the effect of human grief. The face seems
to be almost dissolving in tears while the hands
and teeth create immense tension or anguish.*

Multiple lines of varying length seem to describe the contours of this powerful self-portrait in ink. The technique used is very interesting. Instead of being built up with successive layers of smooth, controlled hatching, the features are drawn with hook-like wiry lines. It's almost as though the artist has drawn directly onto his own face.

Each mark helps to describe the curve of the surface of the facial features. The method is effective because he has not tried to be economical with his lines. The scribbly looking marks used to carefully build up the face give a sort of coarse texture, the effect of which is to increase the feeling of substantiality.

Here Picasso's style is fairly formal but the scratchy, blotty ink technique seems the result of quick drawing of a rather poised subject with little movement in the head itself. The form is realized extremely economically by the splatter of marks, which give a generalized feeling of solidity without any detail. The artist's approach produces a rather statuesque effect.

This head is distorted by its emotional intensity but reads very well as a convincing, solid face and head. Picasso sacrificed accuracy of shape for intensity of feeling and expression. Despite this the head doesn't look unreal and is convincing as a portrayal of powerful emotions in a human face.

EXERCISES: REALIZING FORM
We now look at the sort of exercises that will help you to begin to see how to realize form with some power. They are all difficult but extremely useful and very satisfying when you begin to make them work. It will require repeated practice, of course, but if you want to be an effective artist there is no avoiding hard work.

A geometric pattern on a three-dimensional shape is a marvellous exercise for the draughtsman, and shows how a linear device on a surface can describe the form of that surface.

This tartan-patterned biscuit tin presents various problems. First is drawing the outline with its elliptical top and cylindrical sides. Secondly is the pattern, which proceeds round the curved edge of the tin, but is shown flat on the lid with some perspective.

Draw your outline with the basic pattern inscribed, as shown. Even without the addition of tone or detail, this gives some idea of the roundness of the sides and the flatness of the top.

With this cup and saucer the printed landscape is tricky but interesting. You have to get the details of the printing exactly marked around the curve of the cup, otherwise the cup will look flat. One thing that makes it a bit easier is the fact that some of the details in the pattern are not clear, and so a few mistakes won't necessarily make much difference. The main point to observe is the way the picture reduces in width as it curves around the cup.

The general outline gives the basic shape and some indication of the scene around the curved surfaces of both cup and saucer. But it is not until more detail is added with variations in tone that the roundness of the cup becomes evident.

Another testing exercise is to draw an elderly human face in detail, with all the lines, textures and marks produced by old age. If this is too difficult with a human model (it does take rather a long time and your model may get restless), try drawing from a detailed close-up photograph.

My drawing of the famous pioneer of photography Alfred Stieglitz was done from a photograph taken by one of his pupils. The detail in that original is brilliant and it is quite a tour-de-force to produce it in pencil or ink. When you try it, you'll find that you have to discipline yourself to produce every mark, every little ripple of flesh and tuft of hair with many small careful marks. Allow yourself plenty of time for this exercise.

Human anatomy is perhaps the ultimate test for the draughtsman. If you want to excel at portrait drawing it's worth trying to acquire a skull or the use of one from a medical person or another older artist who might probably have access to one. Carefully draw it from different angles in great detail. Don't hurry, be precise, rub out any mistakes, re-draw ruthlessly and don't be satisfied until the drawing is almost photographic in detail.

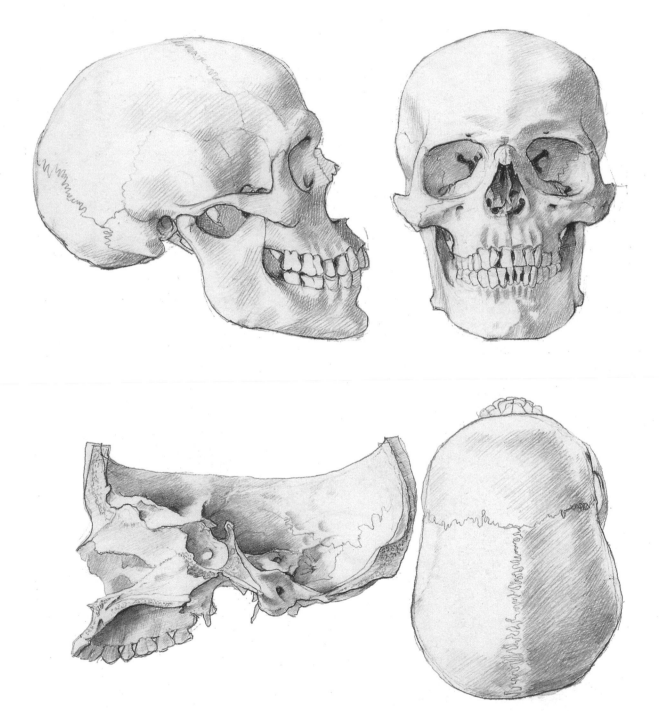

The example shown is a skull that can be taken apart, although in the complete view the lines of division and the hooks that hold the parts together have been left out. The interior of the skull is a particularly tough *challenge because it is unfamiliar to most of us. Keep the drawing precise and clean looking, so that you have no difficulty in seeing where you go wrong. This will make your mistakes easier to correct.*

Assessing What Works

When we embark on designing and drawing a composition, we instinctively look for the best way to express our experience. If we are drawing directly from nature, we may arrange our subject or our own viewpoint in order to get the best possible view.

We may have to alter the lighting with artificial means or move to a position where the light is more conducive to the effect we wish to produce. The object we choose initially for a still life may not be quite right and we may take some time selecting exactly the right one, polishing it, putting it in different positions and generally organizing the shapes to get the best possible arrangement.

A landscape obviously can't be moved around in fact but most artists adjust parts of it to suit their composition. If a tree is in the 'wrong' place it can be left out of the picture or moved around on the canvas without too much difficulty.

When it comes to portraits, apart from getting the best light, background and profile, you can also look at clothes, hairstyle and accessories to make a difference to your composition. The decision to draw just the head, or head and shoulders, half length or full length can also greatly affect the final result.

Every picture needs careful consideration to bring out its full potential. Sometimes you'll find yourself changing your approach at least once to get a drawing right.

EMPHASIS AND LOCATION

Over the next six pages we look at compositional methods over a range of genres from landscape to still life. The examples included are in different styles and in time extend from the Renaissance to the 20th century. All of them contain devices designed to draw you in and ensure you understand the point of the drawing. The diagrams are included to indicate the narrative flow and show you how the visual attention is attracted from one part of a picture to another.

In this straightforward narrative (a copy of Taddeo Gaddi's mural of the Annunciation to the shepherds, in Santa Croce, Florence), we see the shepherds reacting to a bright light in the middle of the picture, on a steeply sloping hill with some trees at the top. In the top right-hand corner there's an area of dark sky and an angel floating out of a brightly-lit cloud, indicating to the shepherds. Down at the bottom, there's a small flock of sheep with a dog looking on. The position of the angel swooping downwards and the shepherds angled across the centre of the picture give an unambiguous, almost strip-cartoon version of the story. The brightness of the angel tells us of his importance, and the position and actions of the shepherds mark them out as central characters. Everything else in the picture is just a frame to convince you that this is outdoors and a fitting context for the shepherds.

This is a copy of a landscape by the 19th-century American painter John Kensett. Rocky wooded banks curve into the picture at about centre-stage. To help the viewer, Kensett has included a group of wildfowl just about to take off from the water. The viewer's attention is immediately grabbed by this movement, and by the detail of the foreground rocks. The inward curve of the water pulls your eyes to the distant mountain peak, rearing up above the surrounding hills. Even the cloudscape helps to frame the rather distinctive mountain, which is on the centre-line. Kensett uses these very precise devices to get us to look at the whole landscape and appreciate the singularity of its features.

The view taken by Degas here is quite extraordinary. We see the upper part of the girl, upside-down as she bends to pick up a sponge. The tub acts as a large, stable base shape and the towel and chair on the floor lead us to the window indicated in the background. Just over half the picture is taken up with this unusual view of quite a simple action and gives an interesting dynamic to the composition. It looks almost as if we have caught sight of this intimate act through an open door. We are close, but somehow detached from the activity, which helps to give the picture a statuesque quality.

Degas has found a very effective way of creating interest just by the arrangement on the canvas. Ordinary, but extra-ordinary.

Like Degas, the American painter Edward Hopper was keen to depict everyday life as he saw it. In this picture, there is no dramatic situation, and not one figure, although the open door suggests that someone may be nearby. The composition is very still, despite the waves on the near surface of the sea glimpsed through the door.

It seems we are looking at a depiction of a timeless summer's day, as experienced in a house by the sea, bright, still, and balanced by the shadow and the light. Despite the simplicity, there is a touch of expectancy, as though someone will soon step into the space. The composition is attention grabbing and oddly peaceful at one and the same time.

The Spaniard Juan Sánchez Cotán found an effective, dramatic way to arrange and light quite ordinary objects in this still life. The dark background, the dangling fruit and cabbage, the cut melon and aubergine on the edge of the ledge produce an almost musical sweep of shapes, all highlighted dramatically. Would Cotán have seen fruit and vegetables arranged like this in late 16th/early 17th century Spain, or did he create this design himself specifically for his painting? Either way, the arrangement is very effective and a brilliant way of injecting drama into quite ordinary subject matter.

We return to Degas to finish this section. We are in a 19th-century dance studio, with a master continuing to instruct his pupils as they rest. All the attention is on the master with his stick, which he uses to beat out the rhythm. The perspective takes you towards him. The way the girls are arranged further underlines his importance. The beautiful casual grouping of the frothy dancers, starting with the nearest and swinging around the edge of the room to the other side, neatly frames the master's figure. He holds the stage.

SYMBOLS AND ASSOCIATIONS

The face is the most obvious barometer of human feeling. However, it is possible to show moods or emotions in other ways – the position or movement of a body can be powerful indicators, for example – and not just rely on the obvious. An even more interesting approach is to let nature be a mirror, and transfer human emotions onto natural features. Consider the examples you will see over the following pages.

The head of Michelangelo's 'David' in Florence symbolizes the defiance of that city towards the hostile autocracies by which it was surrounded. A small but rich and inventive state, Florence was a free republic whose citizens and guilds had a voice in government. Michelangelo's statue of the shepherd boy who kills the giant warrior Goliath is a powerful symbol of the independence of that city and its determination to protect its status.

A breaking wave used as a metaphor for exhilaration is not new. In this example the impact might have been greater and the feeling of exhilaration emphasized if there was a figure of a surfer under the wave.

A beautiful still lake with reflections and calm skies seen in morning or evening light gives the feeling of serenity, especially with the small native boat being propelled smoothly, without haste, across the surface of the water.

This image symbolizes serenity partly by situation and partly by technique. The artist has made efforts to excise any disturbances from the picture.

119

EXTREMES OF EXPRESSIVITY
Here we look at three very different ways of being expressive. The face as a measure of emotional expression is an obvious way to show the mood of a picture by association, but as you will see from these drawings, there are faces and faces. The galloping horse and jockey is a more abstract example of how to produce a visceral response.

Francis Bacon's figures at the base of his 'Three Studies for a Crucifixion' seem to represent a raw, blind fury or perhaps even revenge. Bacon himself identified the figures as representations of the Furies who, in classical myth, torment evil-doers before and after death. Although not classical studies, they seem to apply to classical myth.

Happiness

Intensity

This image is an attempt to convey the idea of speed. The racehorse and jockey are glimpsed pounding down a course, dirt flying up behind. The idea is reinforced by how the image is drawn: the rider with stirrups short, behind raised out of the saddle, the horse's neck stretched, tail streaming, powerful legs bunched up to take the next stride. The economical use of lines also suggests that the image is moving past us at speed.

Satisfaction

Despair

The gentle lyricism in Marc Chagall's drawings could not be further from the feeling of unease, almost revulsion, that we met in Francis Bacon's work. Chagall used a charming, playful way of drawing in much of his work. Most of his paintings have either lyrical or joyful associations in their design, colour or the technique he employed. He chose to portray the magical quality of life and touch our emotions in subtle ways.

Chagall's picture of the circus (opposite) has an almost childlike sense of fun and enjoyment, emphasized by the rather naive handling of the drawing. Everybody seems to be having a good time, even the clowns and acrobats, but without becoming disorderly or too exuberant.

The picture of a poet reclining above, produces an air of gentle melancholy. This is partly due to the rather odd position of the figure, which is lying along the base of the picture, and partly due to the dark trees and almost ghostly toy-like animal shapes grazing in the paddock.

Edvard Munch's 'The Scream' is an expressive and subjective picture that is now read as a general statement about ourselves, particularly the angst and despair experienced by modern man.

The area depicted in the painting was favoured by suicides, and was close to slaughter-houses and a lunatic asylum where Munch's sister was incarcerated.

The artist wrote of the setting: 'the clouds were turning blood red. I sensed a scream passing through nature.'

The original painting has a blood red sunset in steaks of red and yellow, with dark blues and greens and blacks in the large dark areas to the right. The swirling lines and skull-like head with its unseeing eyes and open mouth produce a very strong effect.

'The Kiss', by Viennese artist Gustav Klimt, shows the power of desire in a very graphic manner. The heavily ornamented clothing, while revealing very little of the flesh of the lovers, increases the tactile quality in the work. The firm grasp of the man's hands on the girl's face and head, her hands clinging to his neck and wrist, and her ecstatic expression tell us of the force and intensity of their sexual desire.

Expressing Yourself

All of the images we have looked at in this section try to convey to the viewer a feeling or idea that is not being expressed in words. Indeed, in many of the examples, it would be very difficult to express precisely or concisely the effect they have. One picture can be worth a thousand words. It is not easy to get across a concept by visual means, but with a bit of practice it is possible. Try to produce such an image yourself. You can use or adapt the approaches or methods we've been looking at. When you've produced something, show it to your friends and listen to their reactions. If your attempt is suggestive of the idea you wanted to convey, they will quickly be able to confirm it.

Studying Life from Nature

Throughout history artists have acquired their basic vocabulary through detailed observation of the natural world. Even if the final result in a work is abstracted or manipulated extensively, it is informed by a study of nature.

If you want to make your work convincing, look at the created world around you. Don't view it exclusively through the mediums of photography, television or video. Personal experience will lend a power and knowledge to your work that not only informs you as the artist but also the reviewers of your work. This is very apparent when you look at the work of an artist who has actually experienced at first hand the things he draws. It is also pretty clear to the observant viewer when an artist is only working from second-hand sources, because their drawings tend to lack power.

To achieve realism in your drawings, start by observing plants in detail; even if you live in an urban environment you should be able to find a wide variety to study. You can then move on to animals and human beings. Don't worry about posing them to begin with; just observing them will pay off if you are reasonably systematic about recording what you see so that it remains in your memory.

Observe, too, the effects of light falling on people and objects and how the effects of distance and weather create interesting changes in subject matter. Everything you see and note can be used to advantage in your work. All you need is the time and opportunity to take it all in.

PLANTS AND FLOWERS
The essential structure of a plant is not difficult to see if you study it for a time. Take a group of leaved plants: you soon notice how one type will have leaves in clusters that spring up at the points of the leaves, whereas in another the leaves will hang down around a central point. Some plants have stalks coming off the branches evenly at the same point, others have the stalks staggered alternately down the length of the stem. Once you are familiar with a plant's characteristic shape and appearance, you will begin to notice it or similar properties in other plants. Observation will lend verisimilitude to even your most casual sketches. Look at the examples of plants on this spread, noting their similarities and differences.

The appearance of the Tulip is very formal and upright, with its closed cup-like flower and long stiff stalk and leaves.

The Sedum has a beautiful spiralling arrangement of leaves that curves up into a dish-like form. Rain must fill up the hollow of the leaf and run down the stalk to water the plant's roots.

The leaves of the Hydrangea come off the stem at opposite sides to each other in a symmetrical arrangment. Notice how they curve upwards and then how the curve is reversed, with the upper surface bulging out towards the tip.

The easiest way to study plants is by sketching them as often as you can. Before you begin to draw, look at the plant closely: at the bloom (if there is one), and note how the leaves grow off the stalk. Look at it from above, to see the leaves radiating out from the centre; and from the side to see the different appearance of the leaf shapes as they project towards you, away from you and to each side as they spiral round the stem. Note the texture of the leaves, and how it compares with that of other plants.

When your subject is a flower-head, draw it from an angle, where you can see the pattern of the petals around the centre of the blossom or a profile view of them. Notice the texture of the petals and how the centre of the flower contrasts with the main part of the bloom. When you draw the flower, include a leaf or two to show the contrast in tone or texture between the leaf and the petals.

The delicate blossom of the Camellia looks so fragile. It contrasts beautifully with the solid, perfect shape of the leaves.

The more you draw plants, the more details you will notice and the broader your vocabulary will become. After you have been drawing plants for a while, try drawing one from memory. This type of exercise helps to sustain the image that your senses have recorded and will help you to memorize shapes and textures. You will find drawing from memory gives a simpler result than drawing from life, because you tend to leave out unnecessary details. The ability to produce a conventional shape easily without reference is a great asset. Once you have this ability, you will be able to bring a greater sense of realism to your drawings.

Here we have two blooms from the same plant (a Clematis) at different stages of its growth. The difference is quite dramatic.

The Clematis captured as it is just opening, with its smooth looking petals hanging down.

The fully open bloom, centre showing to the sun. By this stage the edges of the petals are quite crinkly.

PLANTS: GROWTH PATTERNS

Nature offers so much variety, as you will discover once you start studying it in earnest. In the examples shown on this spread you will find three very different effects in as many examples.

Compare them, and note the differences you observe. You will find these patterns of growth fascinating as you investigate them more fully and extend your experience.

The blossom of the Cherry clings closely to the dark stiff, almost spiky branches.

The habit of the Stewartia is to gracefully hold its leaves and small blossoms away from the main branch.

*The acorns and leaves of the
Oak jut out from their stalk.*

Exercising Eye and Hand

It cannot be over-emphasized that, in order to become a proficient artist, you need to get into the habit of drawing every day. If you do, very soon you will become adept at handling almost any shape. Keep trying different objects, and be adventurous, trying more difficult subjects once you've got somewhere with easier ones.

TREES: GROWTH PATTERNS

Drawing trees has always been a favourite pastime of artists even when a commission is not involved. Trees are such splendid plants and often very beautiful but they are not that easy to draw well.

Before you begin, consider the sketches on this page.

Have a look at the bigger trees in your local park or, if you're lucky enough to live out of town, in your local woods and hedgerows. Notice the strength of the root structure when it is evident above ground, like great gnarled hands clutching at the earth. Next, look closely at the bark on the main trunk and branches, then at its texture. Make sketches of what you see.

Oak

Beech

Horse chestnut

SHAPES

Getting a feel for the whole shape of the tree you want to draw is important. Often the best way to approach this is to draw in a vague outline of the main shape first. Then you need to divide this up into the various clumps of leaves and give some indication of how the main branches come off the trunk and stretch out to the final limit of the shape.

Of course, if your subject is a deciduous tree in winter the network of branches will provide the real challenge. The branches are a maze of shapes and success can only be achieved if you manage to analyse the main thrust of their growth and observe how the smaller branches and twigs hive off from the main structure. Luckily trees don't move about too much, and so are excellent 'sitters'.

These three types of deciduous tree present very different shapes and textures. Discover for yourself how different they are by finding an example of each, observing each one closely and then spending time drawing the various shapes. Note the overall shapes and the branch patterns – see accompanying drawings.

Outline of Oak with branch pattern.

Outline of Beech with branch pattern.

Outline of Horse Chestnut showing branch pattern.

133

TREES: PATTERNS

Drawing branches can prove problematical for even experienced artists. The exercise below is designed to get you used to drawing them. Don't worry about rendering the foliage precisely, just suggest it.

I drew this large tree in spring when its leaves were not completely out. It was an ideal subject for demonstrating the intricate tracery of branches because of its position on a wooded slope, which meant that its foliage was largely restricted to the tops of the branches.

When you first look at a tree like this it is not at all easy to see how to pick out each branch. One useful approach is to draw the main stems without initially worrying whether they cross in front of or behind another branch. Only when you draw a branch that crosses the first one need you make a note of whether it crosses behind or in front.

As you add more branches, the depth and space within the tree will become apparent. Ignore any leaves except as vague rounded shapes; you can add them afterwards, if you want.

When seen in silhouette every tree produces a distinctive web pattern. The point of this next exercise is to try to put in as much detail as you can, including leaves (if there are any) and twigs. To achieve this you have to draw the silhouette at a reasonable size; ie, as large as possible on an A4 sheet of paper.

One of the best varieties to choose for this exercise is a Hawthorn, or May, tree. Its twisting, prickly branches and twigs make a really dense mesh, which can be very dramatic. Try drawing it in ink, which will force you to take chances on seeing the shapes accurately immediately; you are committing yourself by not being able to rub out. It won't matter too much if you are slightly inaccurate in detail as long as the main pattern is clear to you.

Winter is the best time to do this exercise, although the worst time to be drawing outdoors. You could, at a pinch, carefully copy a good photograph of such a tree in silhouette, but this would not be such a good test or teach you as much.

This silhouette is rather as you would see it against the sunlight and makes an extraordinary, intricate pattern. There is no problem with the branches being behind or in front of other branches, as there was in the example on the previous page.

135

LOOKING AT THE HEAD

When a person is presented as a subject, the obvious approach is to sit them down in a good light, look at them straight on and begin to draw. However, the obvious does not always produce the best or most accurate result. If you concentrate solely on getting a likeness of a subject, you miss out on the most important and most interesting aspects of portrait drawing.

The aim of this next exercise is to encourage you to look at the head as a whole. There's much more to the head than mere features, as you will discover if you look at it from many different angles, excluding the obvious one. Take a look at the two drawings shown below.

The head leaning back. This angle gives a clear view of underneath the chin and the nose, both areas we rarely notice ordinarily. Seen from this angle the person is no longer instantly recognizable, because the forehead has disappeared and the hair is mostly behind the head.

Notice the large area of neck and chin, and the nostrils, which are coming towards the viewer. See how the nose sticks up out of the main shape of the head. When seen at this angle the ears seem to be in a very odd position, and their placement can be quite tricky. Notice that the eyes no longer dominate the head.

The head looking downwards. This allows a good view of the top of the head, which tends to dominate the area in view. Notice how the eyes disappear partly under the brow; how the eyelashes stick out more noticeably; how the nose tends to hide the mouth and the chin almost disappears.

Once you have looked at various heads of different people you will begin to classify them as whole shapes or structures and not just as faces. This approach teaches that although there are many different faces, many heads share a similar structure. The individual differences won't seem half so important once you realize that there are only a few types of heads and each of us has a type that conforms to one of these.

If you want to fully investigate this phenomenon, get your models to pose with their heads at as many different angles as possible, and explore the structure of what you see. You can use the poses I have provided or create your own.

Mostly when we look at people our attention is too easily captured by the appearance of their eyes and mouth, because these are the principal determiners of facial expression. Once you ignore the facial expression, you *will begin to notice in more detail the shapes of the features. When drawing the head, focus your attention on these features: forehead, jaw, cheekbones and nose. They give the face its structure and thereby its character.*

FIGURE DRAWING: FACIAL FEATURES

The features are worth sketching many times from more than one angle until you begin to understand exactly what happens with every part. You can do this quite easily by just moving your point of view while the model remains still. However, sometimes the head needs to be tilted, the eyes moved and the lips flexed to get a better idea of the way these features change. Time spent working on this now means that your drawing will take on a new conviction in the future and you will begin to notice subtleties that were perhaps less obvious to you before.

Eyes

You will quickly notice that the eye looking up and the eye looking down are vastly different in expression.

The eye seen from below looking up, and seen from above looking up, add extra permutations to the variety of shapes.

See how the eye seen from the side gives a much clearer view of the ball shape and how the lens seems to sit on the surface of the eyeball, the pupil appearing to recede into the shape of the lens.

When the eyes look down the upper eye-lid takes on the shape of the eyeball it is covering and the open part of the eye forms a sort of crescent shape. The upper lid increases and the lower one creases rather.

Ears

Not many people can move their ears, so they are less of a problem than any other feature. Their convolutions are unfamiliar because rarely do we look at them. Seen from the front or back most ears are inconspicuous. The shapes of ears do vary, but have several main shapes in common. Look at these examples.

Nose

The nose doesn't have a great deal of expression although it can be wrinkled and the nostrils flared. However, its shape often presents great difficulty to beginning students. Drawing the nose from in front gives the artist a lot of work to describe the contours without making it look monstrous.

A clear dark shadow on one side helps a lot when drawing the nose from the front.

If you want to reduce the projection of the nose, a full facing light will tend to flatten it in terms of visible contours.

However, from the side it is clear how it is shaped. The nostrils are a well defined part of the nose and from the front are the best part to concentrate on to infer the shape of the rest of the features.

Mouth

The mobility of the mouth ensures that next to the eyes it is the most expressive part of the face. Although there are many different types of mouth, these can be reduced to a few types once you begin to investigate them.

First of all, draw from the front, followed by three-quarter views from left and right, and then from the side.

Next draw from slightly above and slightly below; this gives you the basic shape of the mouth. Note the edge of the lips; some parts project and give a definite edge to the lip. On other parts the colour of the lip is in the same plane as the surface of the face.

When you have a fairly clear idea of the basic form of the mouth, see what happens when it opens. First, try drawing it slightly open from at least two views (front and side) and then wider, and then wide open. Notice what happens to the lips when the mouth is open, how they stretch, and how creases appear in the cheeks either side and below.

Next, look at the mouth smiling; first with the mouth shut, and then more open.

PERSPECTIVE VIEWS: LEGS

One of the most difficult problems with drawing the human figure (or any other figure for that matter) arises when the body or the limbs of the figure being drawn are foreshortened by perspective; an example might be when a leg or arm is projecting towards your viewpoint. Instead of the expected shape of the limb you get an oddly distorted proportion that the mind often wants to correct. However, if you are going to draw accurately, you have to discount what the mind is telling you and observe directly, measuring if necessary to make sure that these rather odd proportions are adhered to. In this way, a limb seen from the end on (as in the illustration right) will carry real conviction with the viewer.

When viewing the leg from the foot end, notice how large the sole of foot looks in comparison with the apparent length of the leg. The muscles and the knee project outwards, their roundness and angularity very pronounced, while their length is reduced to almost nil. If you observe the shapes produced by this view, you shouldn't have any problem. Don't tell yourself that it looks wrong, because it's not; it's just an unusual point of view.

PERSPECTIVE VIEWS: ARMS

The same situation is evident with the arm as with the leg. In this case the size of the hand will often appear outrageously large, practically obscuring the rest of the arm. Seen from this end-on perspective, the bulge of any muscle or bone structure becomes a much more important feature describing the shape of the arm. Instead of a long, slender shape which we recognize as 'arm', we see a series of bumps, rounded shapes, closely stacked up against each other, so that the length of the arm is minimal and the round section of the arm shape becomes what you see and draw.

It will help you make visual sense of a foreshortened hand if you view the limb as though it is one of a group, with the fingers coming off a body (the palm). Take notice of the shapes of the tips of the fingers and the knuckles particularly, because these too will be the dominant features of the fingers seen from end-on.

The shape of the fingernail provides another good clue to seeing the finger as it really is. The main part of the hand loses its dominance in this position but still needs to be observed accurately.

141

HANDS

Hands are relatively easy to study, especially if you use your own as models. If you equip yourself with a mirror you should be able to look at them from almost any angle. Of course, it will also be necessary to look at the hands of an older or younger person and also one of the opposite sex. You will find there are significant differences in shape depending on age and sex.

Always start off by observing the main structure of the hand, based on the bones underneath, and then carefully observe the hardness or softness of the flesh and skin.

The back of the hand gives the clearest indication of the age of your model. Older hands have more protuberant veins and looser, more wrinkled skin around the knuckles. The hands of small children seem smooth all over.

DIFFERENCES IN MUSCULATURE

All human bodies have a tendency towards either a harder or softer muscularity, and both characteristics can make quite a difference to the effect of your finished picture. Look at the examples shown here.

In a hard, muscular body the distinction between the muscles is clear and the angularity of the form has a much more active or even aggressive quality. This quality is accentuated if the bone structure is also prominent. Even in the female figure, which tends to be more restful in shape than the male, when it is lean and bony it has this rather active or awkward look.

A soft, undulating figure, where the differences between the jointing parts of the muscles are not very obvious, gives a very smooth, rounded appearance to the form, and this has an effect of calmness or weightiness. When the flesh is too heavy the weight tends to look more awkward and so is less indicative of calm. Generally, though, softer bodies look more restful than harder ones.

143

FIGURES: COMPOSITION

When it comes to producing drawings of several figures in a composition, the biggest problem, assuming you have had enough experience of drawing live figures, is the way that parts of one figure disappear behind parts of another. Sometimes it is easy to get the composition wrong and end up with an awkward-looking arrangement.

In this simple group of two lovers embracing, compositional success has been achieved by ensuring that the figures combine in such a way that they appear to melt together, with the limbs entwining in a natural way.

When you are posing a picture it is important to be alert to the position of a hand or leg looking awkward. If this happens, try to find the position that is most likely to show the warmth of feeling or the beauty of the pose. In the example shown, notice how the heads relate in such a way that they almost obliterate us, the viewers, from the view.

This drawing of two Victorian wrestlers is based on a painting by William Etty. One figure is being forced down, but the standing figure looks as though it might be levered across from the lower figure's knee. The main point of this picture is the forcefulness of the action and whether the two figures seem to be struggling against each other. Perhaps Leonardo or Michelangelo would give us more expression of the struggle, but nevertheless this composition does evoke the effort that these two strong men are making. The link between the two figures is central to the success of the work.

Two hands clasped give a similar problem to entwined figures in a larger composition. You'll find them easier to tackle if you try to see them as if you were looking at a whole figure.

In this copy of a Caravaggio, the body of Christ is being lifted into its tomb. This event is made interesting and dramatic by the arrangement of the figures and their relationship. The movement of the figure carrying the dead body contrasts starkly with the inert corpse. The limpness of the legs of the dead man contrasts with the gnarled knotty legs of the carrier. The shape made by the man's encircling arms and the bent over figure with his arm under the shoulders and back of Christ are quite complex. Even the strands of grave cloth and the cloak of the younger carrier help to define the activity.

I have omitted from my copy the group of three mourning women which is in the original, because they are not actively engaged in carrying the body.

CLOSE UPS OF JOINTS

When studying the human skeleton or its bones and musculature, it is a good idea at some stage to home in on one joint and draw it in exact detail. Concentrate on making it as anatomically correct as you can, as though you were a draughtsman preparing a specimen for the medical profession.

This sort of detailed study is very effective in making us see more when we come to draw the human figure from life, and it can inform our drawing enormously. There is no substitute for this approach if you want your drawings to carry conviction. The knowledge gained by it seems to go through the hand into the mind, and when we draw it seems to come out again to inform the viewer, even if he has never seen it himself in real life. This is why the works of the old master-draughtsmen still carry so much power.

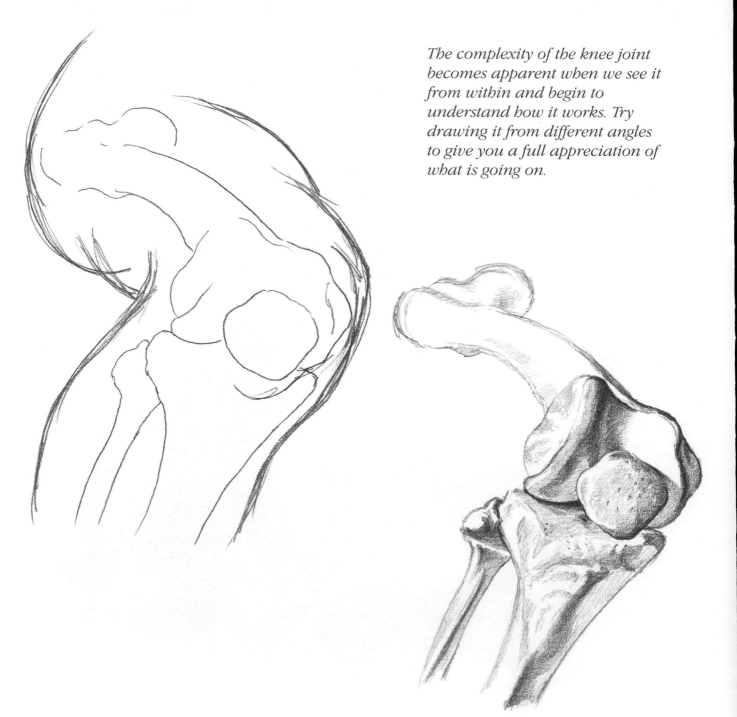

The complexity of the knee joint becomes apparent when we see it from within and begin to understand how it works. Try drawing it from different angles to give you a full appreciation of what is going on.

The hip-joint, where the pelvis and thigh bone rotate, ball in cup, so to speak, has extraordinary flexibility, as detailed study will reveal.

CLOTHING AND MOVEMENT

Next we look at clothing and how the movement and actions of the wearer affect it. Of course, how an item of clothing behaves will depend on the type of material of which it is made, so you need to be aware of different properties and characteristics and how to render them realistically in various situations.

A very simple movement of a girl pulling on her jacket produces all sorts of wrinkles and creases in a rather stiff material. The creases at the bend of the arm are relatively soft, however, which generally indicates an expensive material. As the American Realist painter Ben Shahn, remarked, 'There is a big difference between the wrinkles in a $200 suit and a $1,000 suit.' (This was said in the 1950s, so the prices are relative.) What he was remarking on was the fact that more expensive materials fold and crease less markedly and the creases often fall out afterwards, whereas a suit made of cheaper materials has papery looking creases that remain after the cloth was straightened.

The clothing worn by this figure (right) hangs softly in folds and suggests a lightweight material such as cotton. The shape of the upper body is easily seen but the trousers are thick enough to disguise the shape of the leg.

This drawing (left) was made from a picture of a dancer playing a part. The baggy cotton-like material has a slightly bobbly texture and its looseness in the sleeves and legs serves to exaggerate his movements. Both the action and costume reinforce the effect of floppy helplessness.

A bit of clever posing by a fashion photographer was responsible for the original from which the drawing below was made. The model was actually photographed lying on the floor with the dress spread out to make it look as though she was moving in a smooth-flowing dance. The photograph was taken in the 1930s, before the benefits of high-speed cameras and film, and represents an imaginative way round a technical problem. It proves that you can cheat the eye.

The sturdy girl dancer above is swirling a length of thin, light silken material. The movement of the hair and garment tell you quite a bit about her movements and the materiality of the hair and cloth.

149

Here are three drawings of different types of clothing showing vastly different effects of folds and creases, mainly due to the type of material used in each case.

These jeans, made of tough hard-wearing cotton, crease easily and characteristically, and the creases remain even when the cloth is moved.

A couture garment made of heavy satin and tailored to keep the folds loose and mainly vertical. The movement is not extreme and so the weight and smoothness of the material ensure an elegant effect.

When you come to draw this type of material be sure to get a strong contrast between dark and light to capture the bright reflective quality of the garment.

*The raincoat sleeve shown below is similar in character to
our first example: a stiffish material but one made to repel
water and so has a very smooth sheen. The folds are large,
the sleeve being loose enough to allow ease of movement.
Even in this drawing, they look as though they would
totally disappear when the arm was straightened.*

HAIR

Here is another material associated with the body – hair. We look at two examples and the technical problems involved when trying to draw them. This particular material comes in thin strands that can either curl, tangle or smoothly lay against each other, and these characteristics allow very different qualities to be shown in a drawing. You will find all of these challenging but fascinating to attempt.

The shine on the top of the head shows up strongly, despite the fact of the darkness of the hair. There is also another slightly more subdued shine lower down, across the back of the head. The pleating over, and the plait itself, pick up the shine and accentuate the smooth even strands of hair holding together, none out of place, effectively producing an almost smooth surface to each fold of plait.

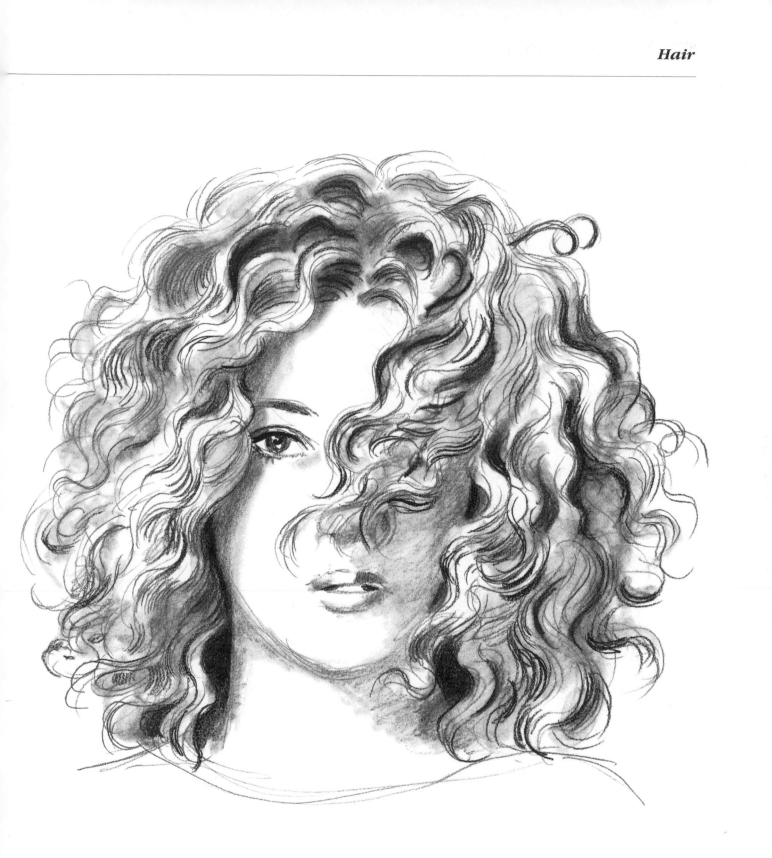

A lot of effort has gone into this hairstyle, with every seemingly wayward strand beautifully arranged. Contrived it may be, but it does show to good effect how hair can wave and corkscrew in ringlets. Notice the

many highlights on the bends of the curls and the darker richer tones underneath. It's not easy to make this style look natural in a drawing, but this is a good attempt.

EARTH

When drawing the solid rocks that make up the surface of the world, it can be instructive to think small and build up. Pick up a handful or soil or gravel and take it home with you for close scrutiny, then try to draw it in some detail. You will find that those tiny pieces of irregular material are essentially rocks in miniature. You can get a very clear idea of how to draw the earth in all its guises by recognizing the essential similarities between earth materials and being prepared to take a jump from almost zero to infinity.

If we attempt to draw a rocky outcrop or the rocks by the sea or along the shore of a river, it is really no different from drawing small pieces of gravel, only with an enormous change of scale. It is as though those pieces of *gravel have been super-enlarged. You will find a similar random mixture of shapes, though made more attractive to our eyes because of the increase in size.*

One more step is to visit a mountainous area and look at the earth in its grandest, most monumental form. This example has the added quality of being above the snow-line and showing marvellously simplified icy structures against contrasting dark rocks.

Now look at a large cliff-face, with its cleavages and striations of geological layering, some of it, no doubt, partially hidden by plants, but nevertheless showing the structure very clearly.

WATER

The character and mood of water changes depending on how it is affected by movement and light. Over the next few pages we look at water in various forms, which present very different problems for artists and very different effects on viewers. To understand how you can capture the effect of each of the forms shown here requires close first-hand study, supported by photographic evidence of what is happening, followed by persistent efforts to draw what you think you know.

A waterfall is an immensely powerful form of water. Most of us don't see such grand works of nature as this magnificent example. Of course, you would need to study one as large as this from a distance to make some sense of it. This drawing is successful largely because the watery area is not overworked, but has been left almost blank within the enclosing rocks, trees and other vegetation. The dark tones of the vegetation throw forward the negative shapes of the water, making them look foaming and fast moving.

Unless you were looking at a photograph, it would be almost impossible to draw with any detail the effect of an enormous wave breaking towards you as you stood on a shore. Leonardo made some very good attempts at describing the movement of waves in drawings, but they were more diagrammatic in form.

This is water as most of us who live in an urban environment see it, still and reflective. Although the surface of a stretch of water may look smooth, usually there is a breeze or currents causing small shallow ripples. Seen from an oblique angle these minute ripples give a slightly broken effect along the edges of any objects reflected in the water. When you draw such a scene you need to gently blur or break the edges of each large reflected tone to simulate the rippling effect of the water.

In this very detailed drawing of a stretch of water rippling gently, there appear to be three different tones for the smooth elliptical shapes breaking the surface. This is not an easy exercise but it will teach you something about what you actually see when looking at the surface of water.

WATER: CONTRASTING MOODS

The contrast in moods between the choppy sea depicted in the first drawing and the glassy looking water in the second couldn't be more extreme. Pay particular attention to the absence of any reflecting light in the first example, and the fact that the second drawing comes across as all-reflection.

In this view of a choppy inky sea, with breaking crests of foam, the skyline is dark and there is no bright reflection from the sky. The shapes of the foaming crests of the wind-blown waves are very important. They must also be placed carefully so that you get an effect of distance, with large shapes in the foreground graduated to smaller and smaller layers as you work your up the page towards the horizon.

Observe how foam breaks; take photographs and then invent your own shapes, once you've seen the typical shapes they make. No two crests of foam are alike, so you can't really go wrong. But, if you are depicting a stormy sea, it is important to make the water between the crests dark, otherwise the effect might be of a bright, albeit breezy, day.

This whole drawing is made up of the sky and its reflection in the river below. The lone boat in the lower foreground helps to give a sense of scale. Although the trees are obviously quite tall in this view, everything is subordinated to the space of the sky, defined by the clouds, and the reflected space in the water. The boat and a few ripples are there to tell the viewer that it is water and not just air. The effect of this vast space and mirror is to generate awe in the viewer.

Practice with Water

Water is one of the most interesting of subjects for an artist to study and certainly adds a lot to any composition. As you will have noticed, the different shapes it can make and the myriad effects of its reflective and translucent qualities are quite amazing. Over the last few pages we've looked at various ways of portraying water but by no means all of them. The subject is limitless, and you will always manage to find some aspect of it that is a little bit different. Go out and find as many examples as you can to draw.

THE SKY: CONTRASTS

Air is invisible, of course, so cannot really be drawn, but it can be inferred by looking at and drawing clouds and skyscapes. Whether fluffy, ragged, streaky or layered, clouds give a shape to the movements of the elements in the sky and are the only visible evidence of air as a subject to draw.

Here we see dark, stormy clouds with little bits of light breaking through in areas around the dark grey. The difficulty is with the subtle graduations of tone between the very heavy dark clouds and the parts where the cloud cover is thinner or partly broken and allows a gleam of light into the scene. Look carefully at the edges of the clouds, how sometimes they are very rounded and fluffy and sometimes torn and ragged in shape. If you get the perspective correct, they should be shown as layers across the sky, flatter and thinner further off and as fuller more rolling masses closer to. You can create a very interesting effect of depth and space across the lower surfaces of the cloudscape with bumps and layers of cloud that reduce in depth as they approach the horizon.

When the clouds allow more sun to shine through, they look much less heavy and threatening and often assume quite friendly looking shapes. Essentially, though, it is the same vapour as in the stormy sky but with more light, enabling us to see its ephemeral nature.

The effect of beams of sunlight striking through clouds has a remarkable effect in a picture, and can give a feeling of life and beauty to even a quite banal landscape.

A lot has been achieved here with very simple means. The clouds are not complicated and it is the sun's rays (marked in with an eraser) and the aircraft that do much of the work, giving the illusion of height and also limitless space above our view. The broken light, the light and dark clouds and sunlight glinting against the wings and fuselage of the aircraft give the drawing atmosphere.

THE SKY: USING SPACE

The spaces between clouds as well as the shapes of clouds themselves can alter the overall sense we get of the subject matter in a drawing. The element of air gives us so many possibilities, we can find many different ways of suggesting space and open views. Compare these examples.

This open flat landscape with pleasant soft-looking clouds gives some indication of how space in a landscape can be inferred. The fluffy cumulus clouds floating gently across the sky gather together before receding into the vast horizon of the open prairie. The sharp perspective of the long, straight road and the car in the middle distance tell us how to read the space. This is the great outdoors.

162

Another vision of air and space is illustrated here: a sky of ragged grey and white clouds, and the sun catching distant buildings on the horizon of the flat, suburban heathland below. Note particularly the low horizon, clouds with dark, heavy bottoms and lighter areas higher in the sky.

Despite the presence of dark, dramatic clouds in this scene at sunset the atmosphere is not overtly gloomy or brooding. The bright sun, half-hidden by the long flat cloud, radiates its light across the edges of the clouds, which tell us that they are lying between us and the sun. The deep space between the dark layers of cloud gives a slightly melancholic edge to the peacefulness.

Extremes of Expression

Artists in all ages have been interested in extremes of expression and experimenting with the handling of grotesque or humorous depictions of faces and bodies. In the medieval period, they were almost exclusively to be found in sculpture within and without chapels and cathedrals. Look at the misericords, or brackets, on the underside of any seat in choir stalls of this period and you will often find grotesque and fantastic carvings. Similarly the stone gargoyles or spouts which carry water clear of the sides of buildings were often sculpted to resemble the heads of beasts or monsters.

When we get to the Renaissance period, celebrated artists such as Leonardo were drawing grotesque faces and heads, and in some instances taking them to fantastic extremes. The development of printing techniques enabled artists with a social or political message to take caricature beyond the realms of pure fun. William Hogarth, who trained as an engraver before he studied painting, campaigned vigorously against a number of social ills through his work. Later social caricaturists, such as Thomas Rowlandson and James Gillray, went even further in their efforts to change opinion. Their lampoons were reproduced extensively and sold in the streets. Both men were very accomplished artists.

In the 19th century, with the quick delivery of newspapers all over the country, caricature took off in a big way. The satirical weekly newspaper *Punch*, which first appeared in 1841, was packed full of unflattering depictions of leading politicians and other visual comments on scandals, political manoeuvrings and social injustice. In our own time the production of cartoons on film has led to the extension of the art to television.

Inexperienced artists try so hard to be technically correct that often they turn out drawings that look wooden and lack expression. Caricature is a great antidote, helping to free us from an over-reliance on accuracy and to find a genuine means of expression in our work.

GROTESQUES TO FANTASY

Leonardo da Vinci has left us many extraordinary examples of caricature which are undoubtedly not true to life but still recognizable. No one knows why the great man was so fascinated by this type of drawing but perhaps it is not surprising he wanted to see how far he could go with it.

In the second half of the 16th century the Milanese painter Giuseppe Arcimbaldo took caricature in a different direction, producing fantasy portrait heads in which the features were composed of clusters of fruit and vegetables. Some later commentators considered him to be an ancestor of the Surrealists.

Examples from both artists are seen here.

The features of this man (original by Leonardo) are greatly exaggerated and can in no way be taken as realistic – nose protuding, mouth pushed up at the centre and down at the sides. The great lump of a chin completes the ludicrous effect, which glazed eyes and rather lumpy ears don't diffuse.

This second copy of a Leonardo is more realistic apart from the protruding jaw which is taken to unnatural lengths. The first face looked rather stupid; this one looks more intelligent and even kindly.

This extraordinary face by Arcimbaldo is reputed to be of the Hapsburg Emperor Rudolph II. Although made up of fruit and vegetables it is easily readable as a particular *human face. The drawing is an amusing conceit but one doesn't know whether it was meant to make fun of its subject or was just a curious exercise in ingenuity.*

167

CARICATURE AS SATIRE

The work of the great caricaturists was born out of social and political turmoil. Hogarth, Rowlandson and Gillray, three of Britain's greatest exponents of caricature, came to the fore at a time of unprecedented change. All three were valued more for their caricaturing skills than their serious gifts, an oversight that was particularly hard on Hogarth, who was undoubtedly a major artist.

In Spain, Francisco Goya was also railing against the injustices and follies he saw around him. He chronicled the horrors of the occupation by Napoleon's armies in both paint and ink. In his smaller studies we get snapshots of the human condition in extremes of expression that ring true.

Hogarth's view of the journalist and political agitator John Wilkes.

A money-lender as seen through the sharp eye of Rowlandson.

In his series of drawings known as 'Los Caprichos', Goya castigated a host of iniquities. Here it is the Catholic Church, represented by two rather disreputable looking monks.

At the end of the 18th century Napoleon became a target for English caricaturists, who, like their countrymen, feared what might happen once he had overrun mainland Europe. Initially portrayed by them as a tiny monkey-like character with a big hat, he evolved into a portly villain with a scowl and a big chin.

No one was safe from the caricaturists' pen, even the Duke of Wellington, a great hero of the popular press thanks to his victories in the Napoleonic Wars. The treatment of him in these two contemporary examples, after he had swapped his uniform for a frock coat and entered Parliament, is fairly good natured.

Political leaders at home came in for just as much attack from the caricaturists as their foreign counterparts.

In these two examples (above) it is a weasely-looking William Pitt the Younger by Gillray. Fresh-faced in the first illustration (he was after all only 24 when he became British Prime Minister for the first time), he seems to have matured a little in the second, with clusters of freckles on the nose and cheek and the makings of a moustache and beard.

Pitt's great political rival, Charles James Fox, by Rowlandson.

CARICATURE AS ART

In 19th-century France political comment was often mixed with an illustrative kind of art which combined to make a rather strange brew. The result was certainly caricature but of a type that was more finished and obviously polished. The Salon culture of the French art world would have been horrified by less. The influence of the Impressionists would soon be felt, however, even in caricature.

Honoré Daumier made many drawings which hovered at the edges of caricature. The first of the two examples of his work shown here is from a French treatise on suffrage. The second, taken from a journal, is of 19th century France's leading literary figure, Victor Hugo, hence the immense brow.

Jean-Louis Forain was a regular contributor to journals as a caricaturist and graphic artist. This example of his work shows a departure in style from the satirical drawing usually seen in France up to this time. Very few lines have been used to depict the sleek, moustachioed bourgeois gentleman in evening dress.

An early caricature by Impressionist Claude Monet of his art teacher.

A contemporary of Forain, Arthur Rackham became popular for his book illustrations, especially of children's stories. Rackham's imaginative approach went down well not only with children, who were sometimes almost frightened by them, but by their parents who particularly admired his finely drawn grotesquerie.

171

STEREOTYPING

All the well-known public figures of the last fifty years or so are mostly remembered by us because we are familiar with caricature images of them we have seen in newspapers and magazines and on films and television.

As well as emphasizing perceived personal weaknesses or humorous aspects of public figures, caricature can also be used creatively to suggest solid virtues, such as those of perhaps the two most famous national stereotypes of all time, Uncle Sam and John Bull.

A century separates the creation of Uncle Sam (c. 1812) and John Bull (c.1712), the one epitomizing the US government and the other the average British citizen.

The great dictators of the 20th century are rather better known by their cartoon image than their real faces.

Hitler   *Mussolini*   *Stalin*   *Mao*

MODERN TRENDS

The modern trend in caricature is to fix on one or two obvious physical characteristics and subordinate everything else to the effect these create. Presenting an absolute minimum likeness can only work, of course, if an audience is very familiar with the figures depicted. In the following examples, aimed at a British market, note that the caricatures of the two lesser known figures, Murdoch and Le Pen, are more carefully drawn than the others.

Former British Prime Minister Tony Blair and his wife, Cherie.

Former US President Bill Clinton.

Australian media tycoon Rupert Murdoch.

French right-wing politician Jean-Marie Le Pen (after Gerald Scarfe).

BUILDING A CARICATURE
The process of turning a perfectly normal looking person into a cartoon figure to accentuate their traits is the same whether the subject is familiar to millions of households or just one. It can be a fun exercise. The subject I have chosen here is my eldest son. His features are perfectly normal, but as I know quite a lot about him I can accentuate certain areas to bring out his personality to the casual observer. Let's begin the process.

1. It is a good idea first to draw the person you wish to caricature several times, to get to know the shapes of their features and how these relate to each other.

2. I have slightly exaggerated his way of staring intensely, his bony physiognomy, strong jaw. I've also tried to suggest his height (6ft 4in).

3. Here I begin to produce something like a caricature. Notice how I have made him grin, although he wasn't doing this when I drew him. People who know him are familiar with his broad, up-turning grin, intense stare, large bony forehead, nose, cheekbones and jaw, and these are the characteristics I have tried to bring out.

1.

2.

3.

EXPERIMENTING

I could have taken that final illustration further and gone on until all superfluous lines had been deleted. You can do this more effectively if you know your subject well. You need knowledge to be able to build into your caricature attitudes, movements and favourite expressions in order to inject a bit of humour as well as get across a likeness with a minimum of detail.

Here are two examples for you to experiment with and see how far you can take the exaggeration before the subject becomes unrecognizable. Try to capture the obvious features first and then the general effect of the head or face.

Don't try caricaturing your friends, unless you don't mind losing them or they agree. If you can't get the subject you want to pose for you, try to obtain good photographs of them. These won't provide quite such good reference, but as long as you draw on your knowledge of the person as well, they should be adequate.

IDENTIFYING FEATURES:
1. *Round head*
2. *Fat chin*
3. *Grim mouth*
4. *Heavy, anxious eyebrows*
5. *Little eyes with bags*
6. *Blobby or broken nose*
7. *Wrinkles and unshaven chin*

Normal   *Exaggerated*

IDENTIFYING FEATURES:
1. *Round-ended, turned-up nose*
2. *Bright eye*
3. *Thick eyebrows*
4. *Big hair on top*
5. *Chin*
6. *Cheeky grin*

Normal   *Exaggerated*

Styles and Techniques

To develop an individual style and method of working, you have to experiment. This is quite easy, given the wide range of materials and implements available. Next, we consider different implements and papers and the effects that can be achieved with them – for example, various types of pencil, as well as pen and ink, line and wash, chalk, pastel and charcoal. We also look at scraper-board, a technique not used very much these days, and some rather interesting if labour-intensive ways of making marks on paper.

In addition we look at some of the approaches to the art of drawing taken by different artists at different times. Some of these may seem alien or too different from the way of working you are used to. Don't be concerned if this is the case. Experimentation gives us the opportunity to discover new techniques and approaches, and to incorporate them in our work. Do try your hand at all of them, and see if you can invent a new style. The main point is to have some fun.

IMPLEMENTS AND MATERIALS

The implements we draw with are important, as is the material we draw on. A keen artist will draw with anything and make it work to his advantage. Artists have to draw, no matter the situation they are in. If nothing else is available, they'll use sticks in sand, coal on whitewashed walls, coloured mud on flat rocks – anything to be able to draw. If you don't have a wide range of equipment at your disposal, don't let that stop you. Use whatever is to hand. However, if at all possible, supply yourself with the best materials you can afford. If you try as many new tools and materials as you can, you will discover what suits you best. Here are some obvious basic implements.

Pencil

The simplest and most universal tool of the artist is the humble pencil, which is very versatile. It ranges from very hard to very soft and black (H, HB, B, 2B, etc.) and there are differing thickness. Depending on the type you choose, pencil can be used very precisely and also very loosely.

You should have at least three degrees of blackness, such as an HB (average hardness and blackness), 2B (soft and black) and 4B (very soft and black).

For working on a toned surface, you might like to try white carbon pencil.

Graphite

Graphite pencils are thicker than ordinary pencils and come in an ordinary wooden casing or as solid graphite sticks with a thin plastic covering. The graphite in the plastic coating is thicker, more solid and lasts longer, but the wooden casing probably feels better. The solid stick is very versatile because of the actual breadth of the drawing edge, enabling you to draw a line a quarter of an inch thick, or even thicker, and also very fine lines. Graphite also comes in various grades, from hard to very soft and black.

Charcoal

Charcoal pencils in black and grey and white are excellent when you need to produce dimensional images on toned paper and are less messy to use than sticks of charcoal and chalk. However, the sticks are more versatile because you can use the long edge as well as the point. Drawings in this type of media need 'fixing' to stop them getting rubbed off, but if interleaved with pieces of paper they can be kept without smudging. Work you wish to show for any length of time should be fixed with spray-can fixative.

Chalk

This is a cheaper and longer-lasting alternative to white conté or white pastel.

Pen

Push-pens or dip-pens come with a fine pointed nib, either stiff or flexible, depending on what you wish to achieve. Modern fine-pointed graphic pens are easier to use and less messy but not so versatile, producing a line of unvarying thickness. Try both types.

The ink for dip-pens is black 'Indian ink' or drawing ink; this can be permanent or water-soluble.

Brush

A number 0 or number 2 nylon brush is satisfactory for drawing. For applying washes of tone, a number 6 or number 10 brush either in sablette or sable or any other material capable of producing a good point is recommended.

Paper and board

Any decent smooth cartridge paper is suitable for drawing. A rougher surface gives a more broken line and greater texture. Try out as many different papers as you can. For brushwork, use a modestly priced watercolour paper to start with. Most line illustrators use a smooth board but you may find this too smooth and your pen sliding across it so easily that your line is difficult to control.

Scraper-board has a layer of china-clay which is thick enough to allow dry paint to be scraped off but thin enough not to crack off. It comes in black and white. White scraper-board is the more versatile of the two, and allows the ink to be scraped with a sharp point or edge when it is dry to produce interesting textures or lines. The black version has a thin layer of black ink printed evenly over the whole surface which can be scraped away to produce a reverse drawing resembling a woodcut or engraving. Try them out. Cut your first piece of board into smaller pieces so that you can experiment with a range of different approaches. (The more unusual techniques involving scraper-board are dealt with later in this section.)

The tools you need to work effectively with scraper-board can be obtained at any good art or craft shop.

Pencils
HB B 2B 4B

Conté charcoal pencil

White carbon pencil

Graphite pencils

Fine line pen

Fine nib push pen

White chalk

Conté stick

Willow charcoal

No 5 sable brush

No 2 nylon brush

Scraper-board tool

Clutch pencil with silver wire point

Ordinary hand-held sharpeners won't always take the thickness of lead in a graphite pencil. A craft knife, though, gives a very good point.

Drawing ink

PENCIL DRAWING

Pencil can be used in many ways. When it was invented – sometime in the 17th century – it revolutionized artists' techniques because of the enormous variety of skilful effects that could be produced with it, and soon came to replace well established drawing implements such as silver-point.

The production of pencils in different grades of hardness and blackness greatly enhanced the medium's versatility. Now it became easy to draw in a variety of ways: delicately or vigorously, precisely or vaguely, with linear effect or with strong or soft tonal effects.

Here we have several types of pencil drawing, from the carefully precise to the impulsively messy, from powerful, vigorous mark making to soft, sensitive shades of tone.

Michelangelo is a good starting point for ways of using pencil. His work was extremely skilful and as you can see from this drawing his anatomical knowledge was second to none. The careful shading of each of the muscle groups in the body gives an almost sculptural effect, which is not so surprising when you consider that sculpture was his first love. To draw like this takes time and patience and careful analysis of the figure you are drawing.

Titian's drawing, however, is quite different. This artist's knowledge of colour was so good that even his drawings look as though they were painted. He is obviously feeling for texture and depth and movement in the space and is not worried about defining anything too tightly. The lines merge and cluster together to make a very powerful tactile group.

Now look at this vigorous drawing by Delacroix, the great French Romantic artist. The powerful flowing lines show the activity and forcefulness of the figure. Where shading has been applied it is very strongly blocked in areas of dark shadows.

Handling pencil in this way requires confidence. When you are learning it is useful sometimes just to let go and have a shot at producing a strong image. You have nothing to lose – you can always have another go if your drawing goes wrong.

PRECISION

In these examples the pencil is used almost scientifically with the line taking pre-eminence. Sometimes it is used to produce an exact effect of form, sometimes to show the flow and simplicity of a movement.

This meticulous pencil drawing, by the German Julius Schnorr von Carolsfeld, is one of the most perfect drawings in this style I've ever seen. The result is quite stupendous, even though this is just a copy and probably doesn't have the precision of the original. Every line is visible. The tonal shading which follows the contours of the limbs is exquisitely observed. This is not at all easy to do and getting the repeated marks to line up correctly requires great discipline. It is worth practising this kind of drawing because it will increase your skill at manipulating the pencil and test your ability to concentrate.

THE SIMPLE OUTLINE

In different ways all the drawings on this page use a simple outline. Such simplicity serves to 'fix' the main shape of the drawing, ensuring the effect of the additional detailed shading.

A much more economical method of drawing has been used for two of the drawings here, but note that this has not been at the expense of the information offered about the subjects depicted.

Both Matisse (copy of a self-portrait, above) and Victor Ambrus (left) appear to have used several different grades of pencil for these drawings; some lines are very soft and black, others much less so. Knowing how far to go is an art in itself. Ambrus has achieved balance by outlining the main shape of the dog with a soft grey line and then adding details of the curly hair and dark ears, head and nose with darker, crisper lines.

Only one of the objects in this still-life group has been drawn in great detail. The rest of them are in a bare outline drawing. This is an unfinished drawing but does show how to achieve a convincing solidity by first drawing clearly defined outline shapes before leaping in at the deep end with detailed drawing.

PEN AND INK

Pen and ink is special in that once you've put the line down it is indelible and can't be erased. This really puts the artist on his mettle because, unless he can use a mass of fine lines to build a form, he has to get the lines 'right' first time. Either way can work.

Once you get a taste for using ink, it can be very addictive. The tension of knowing that you can't change what you have done in a drawing is challenging. When it goes well, it can be exhilarating.

Leonardo probably did the original of this as a study for a painting. Drawn fairly sketchily in simple line, it shows a young woman with a unicorn, a popular courtly device of the time. The lines are sensitive and loose but the whole hangs together very beautifully with the minimal of drawing. The curving lines suggest the shape and materiality of the parts of the picture, the dress softly creased and folded, the face and hand rounded but firm, the tree slightly feathery looking. The use of minimal shading in a few oblique lines to suggest areas of tone is just enough to convey the artist's intentions.

This copy of a Raphael is more heavily shaded in a variety of cross-hatching, giving much more solidity to the figures despite the slightly fairy-tale imagery. The movement is conveyed nicely, and the body of the rider looks very substantial as he cuts down the dragon. The odd bits of background lightly put in give even more strength to the figures of knight, horse and dragon.

This next copy, of a Michelangelo drawing, is much more heavily worked over, with hefty cross-hatching capturing the muscularity of the figure. The texture is rich and gives a very good impression of a powerful, youthful figure. The left arm and the legs are unfinished but even so the drawing has great impact.

Rarely have I seen such brilliant line drawing in ink of the human figure as those of the painter Guercino. In this example the line is extremely economical and looks as though it has been drawn from life very rapidly. The flowing lines seem to produce the effect of a solid body in space, but they also have a marvellous lyrical quality of their own. Try drawing like this, quickly without worrying about anything except the most significant details, but getting the feel of the subject in as few lines as possible. You will have to draw something directly from life in order to get an understanding of how this technique works.

In his masterly original of this drawing in line (and ink), Tintoretto was careful to get the whole outline of the figure. The curvy interior lines suggest the muscularity of the form. There is not too much detail but just enough to convince the eye of the powerful body; every muscle here appears to ripple under the skin. The barest of shading suggests the form.

PRACTISING WITH PEN AND INK

The drawings on this page show what can be achieved with pens of different nib thickness. The series of heads shows the effect that can be achieved with a fine nib. The mass of lines going in many directions give a definite impression of solidity as well as depth of shadows and light.

The figure of the boy is drawn with a felt tip pen. This is not the most sensitive of tools but as long as you don't expect too much from it as a medium, it does enable you to draw quickly and reasonably effectively.

The heads of the boy and girl show the importance of background when attempting to describe the way form builds around a rounded object. Some areas have been left clear to suggest light catching the hair, ears, nose, etc., and these stand out against the cross-hatched background tone.

To practise this technique, try it on small

areas initially. The aim is to learn to control your pen strokes so that you can lay them closely together without them becoming jumbled. You will need several attempts to make the lines only go over the areas you want them to. Try drawing in the main shape with pencil first and then ink over it so that you have pencil lines to draw up to.

The thickness of felt tip pen limits your options so far as size is concerned. As you can see here, you have to draw bigger or reduce areas of tone to their simplest.

This copy of a head by Matisse is remarkably freely drawn and yet the multiple lines build up into a dense texture of materiality that looks very convincing.

PRACTICE

This set of women's heads gives you a chance to try different methods of using line in pen and ink. All methods are possible and can be used to good effect. Think about your lines first, before laying them down in pencil. Look at my notes first before you begin to attempt to draw them.

1. With its fairly solid black lines and simplification of form, this drawing resembles a woodcut. Just a fine line suggests roundness of form.

2. Curved, loosely drawn lines without any tone are used here, to give maximum effect for minimal drawing. A flexible pen nib is necessary to get slightly broader and also finer lines alternating. Note the simplicity of the facial features.

3. Even the outlined frame adds to the decorative effect of this drawing. The intensely layered curls on the head make a pattern rather than a realistic effect, as does the pleated collar around the shoulders. The face is sharply drawn but without much attempt at form. The large areas of white shoulders and neck and blank background help to emphasize the decorative quality of the drawn parts.

4. The face here is again economically drawn: just two black eyes, and mere touches for the nose and mouth. The hair outlining the face and neck, though, has been rendered as a jungle-like mass of black lines overlaying each other. Slightly more formal lines in the background allow the hair to fade into the paper and emphasize the paleness of the face.

5. This drawing is also mostly concerned with the decorative effect of the precisely waved lines of hair, crossed by the carefully delineated pearl head-dress, all flatly drawn with the clear sharp lines reminiscent of an engraving. The dots that make up the background are carefully spaced to ensure that one area is not darker than another. Against this darker background the sharply drawn profile and eyes appear almost in silhouette. No attempt has been made to produce depth of form.

1.

2.

3.

4.

5.

6.

The joy of drawing like this comes in making patterns of the lines and dots, and because this can't be hurried, it is very therapeutic.

6. This head is similar to the third one in that the hair and collar of the dress are carefully built up patterns to suggest an ornate hair-do and an elegant negligée. The difference between the two drawings is mainly in the background. In this drawing there is no obvious perspective. The squares within squares suggest there must be depth behind the head.

189

LINE AND WASH

Now we move on to look at the effects that can be obtained by using a mixture of pen and brush with ink. The lines are usually drawn first to get the main shape of the subject in, then a brush loaded with ink and water is used to float across certain areas to suggest shadow and fill in most of the background to give depth.

A good-quality solid paper is necessary for this type of drawing; try either a watercolour paper or a very heavy cartridge paper. The wateriness of the tones needs to be calculated to the area to be covered. In other words, don't make it so wet that the paper takes ages to dry.

This copy of a Rembrandt is very dramatic in its use of light and shade.

When using line and wash in landscape drawing, the handling of the wash is particularly important, because its different tonal values suggest space receding into the picture plane. Here we look at three drawings by Claude Lorrain.

This sensitive pen line drawing of part of an old Roman ruin has a light wash of watery ink to suggest the sun shining from behind the stones. The wash has been kept uniform. The outlines of the stone blocks give you lines to draw up to.

These two deer are fairly loosely drawn in black chalk. A variety of tones of wash has been freely splashed across the animals to suggest form and substance.

This purely wash drawing of the Tiber at Rome has a few small speckles of pen work near the horizon. The tones vary from very pale in the distance to gradually darkening as we approach the foreground, which is darkest of all. The dark tone is relieved by the white patch of the river, reflecting the light sky with a suggestion of reflection in a softer tone. A brilliant sketch.

Master landscape painter Claude Lorrain gives a real lesson in how to draw nature in this study of a tree. Executed with much feeling but great economy, the whole drawing is done in brushwork.

To try this you need three different sizes of brush (try Nos. 0 or 1, and 6 and 10), all of them with good points. Put in the lightest areas first (very dilute ink), then the medium tones (more ink less water), and then the very darkest (not quite solid ink).

Notice how Lorrain doesn't try to draw each leaf, but makes interesting blobs and scrawls with the tip of the brush to suggest a leafy canopy. With the heavier tones he allows the brush to cover larger areas and in less

detail. He blocks in some very dark areas with the darkest tone and returns to the point of the brush to describe branches and some clumps of leaf.

192

CHALK ON TONED PAPER

The use of toned paper can bring an extra dimension to a drawing and is very effective at producing a three-dimensional effect of light and shade. Whether you are drawing with chalk, pastel or charcoal it is very important to remember that the paper itself is in effect an implement, providing all the tones between the extremes of light and dark. You must resist the temptation to completely obliterate the toned paper in your enthusiasm to cover the whole area with chalk marks. Study the following examples.

This head is drawn simply in a medium toned chalk on a light paper. Here the challenge is not to overdo the details. The tones of the chalk marks are used to suggest areas of the head, and definite marks have been kept to a minimum.

The mid-tone of the paper has been used to great effect in this copy of Carpaccio's drawing of a Venetian merchant. Small marks of white chalk pick out the parts of garments, face and hair that catch the light. No attempt has been made to join up these marks. The dark chalk has been used similarly: as little as the artist felt he could get away with. The medium tone of the paper becomes the solid body that registers the bright lights falling on the figure. The darkest tones give the weight and the outline of the head, ensuring that it doesn't just disappear in a host of small marks.

As we have seen in the examples on the previous spread, the use of toned paper reduces the area that has to be covered in chalk and heightens the effect of the chalk marks, especially if these have been made in white. The three illustrations shown here exemplify the range of effects that can be achieved with toned paper.

In Watteau's picture of a goddess (left) the dark outline emphasizes the figure and limbs, as do the patches of bright light on the upper facing surfaces.

The two drawings shown on this page were executed in white and dark chalk on medium toned paper. The approach taken with the first is about as economical as you can get. The form of the surface of the girl's face and figure is barely hinted at down one side, with just the slightest amount of chalk. A similar effect is achieved on the other side, this time in dark chalk. The uncovered paper does much of the rest of the work.

The second drawing takes the use of dark and light much further, creating a substantial picture. In places the white chalk is piled on and elsewhere is barely visible. The dark chalk is handled in the same way. More of the toned paper is covered, but its contribution to the overall effect of the drawing is not diminished for that.

The French neo-classicist master Pierre Paul Prud'hon was a brilliant worker in the medium of chalk on toned paper. In these copies of examples of his work, he shows us two very effective ways of using light and dark tones to suggest form.

In this drawing of Psyche, marks have been made with dark and light chalk, creating a texture of light which is rather Impressionistic in flavour. The lines, which are mostly quite short, go in all directions.

The impression created is of a figure in the dark. This is helped by the medium tone of the paper, which almost disappears under the pattern of the mark making.

The chalk marks in this close up are very disciplined. A whole range of tones is built from the carefully controlled marks, which show up the form as though lit from above. Here, too, the middle tone is mostly covered over with gradations of black and white.

SCRAPER-BOARD TECHNIQUE

Scraper-board drawing evolved during the early days of photographic reproduction in newspapers as a response to the needs of advertisers, who wanted to show their wares and products to best advantage but were limited by the poor quality of the printing processes then available. The technique gave very clear, precise definition to photographs, and so became the means of rendering advertisements for newsprint. Over time, of course, the screen printing of photographs improved so much that it has become just another art technique. Scraper-board does have some qualities of its own, however. It is similar in some respects to wood engraving, wood cuts or engraving on metal, although because of the ease of drawing it is more flexible and less time-consuming.

In this drawing the boatman appearing across a misty lake or river was first sketched in pencil, then blocked out in large areas of ink. The figure of the man, the oars and the atmospherics were done in diluted ink to make a paler tone. The boat was drawn in black ink. Using a scraper-board tool, lines were carefully scratched across the tonal areas, reducing their tonal qualities further. Some areas have few or no scratched lines, giving a darker tone and an effect of dimensionality.

You can see in the two examples below how scraper-board technique lends itself to a certain formalized way of drawing. The scratch marks can be made to look very decorative. The Christmas Card drawing and lettering is in a very similar technique and has been produced using both scraper-board and pen and ink. The main effort is taken up with making the shapes decorative and giving the main lines a textural quality; this is achieved by using either a brush or the side of a flexible nib.

The top illustration was first drawn in black ink. The areas of ink were then gone over using the scraper tool to reduce the heaviness of the shaded areas and clean up the edges to achieve the shape required.

The Christmas card drawing is mainly thick line in brush with a few lines in pen added afterwards to provide details. The scraper tool was then used to sharpen up the outline and the spaces between the areas of black.

Using the Technique

Scraper-board technique is similar to cross-hatching with a pencil, although with the former you are drawing white on black, of course. The surface of the board can be scratched over several times, as long as the marks have not cut too deeply into the china clay. Any area that needs to be strengthened or corrected can be filled in with ink. Correcting lines using this technique is very easy: you just scratch out the wrong bits and redraw them.

MERRY CHRISTMAS

BLOTTING TECHNIQUE

First used by illustrators in the 1950s, this technique was made famous by Andy Warhol in his fashion illustrations. The idea is to take a piece of ordinary cartridge paper, or blotting paper – either will achieve the same effect – and fold it in half. After drawing each line in ink you blot it into the opposite side of the page (see illustrations below). You have to take a painstaking approach, blotting as you build up the drawing, because otherwise the ink dries too quickly. A dip-pen is the best tool, because modern graphic pens don't produce ink that is wet enough.

1. Draw a line.

2. Fold paper over to blot the ink on the opposite side.

3. Draw your next line and repeat the procedure, folding your paper over to blot the ink on the opposite side.

Producing an Effect

Generally it is best to draw only a few lines at a time and then blot them immediately. If you draw too many lines before blotting them the ink will dry and the point of using this technique will be lost. However, you have to experiment with timings and weight of line, because sometimes a pleasing effect can result from an unpromising start. In the last drawing on the opposite page, for example, the multiple lines on the face dried so quickly that the blotted version looked much less tonal than the original. I liked the effect, though, and didn't try to change it. How you want your finished drawing to look is up to you.

Original drawing   *Blotted version*

Original drawing   *Blotted version*

Original drawing   *Blotted version*

CARD-EDGE TECHNIQUE

This technique was invented at about the same time as the blotting technique we've just looked at. The first step is to cut out small pieces of card. The edges of these are then dipped into soft wet paint (gouache designer colours are best) and used to draw lines onto a blank sheet. The effect is initially very strong, becoming fainter and fainter as the paint gets used up or dries.

Like blotting technique, it is a slow process and you cannot produce much in the way of curved shapes, but the end result can be very powerful. In terms of how it is used and the effects that can be achieved with it, it is rather similar to painting with a palette knife.

In this example the gouache on the edge of the card was almost dry when it was used to paint the clouds and front surface of the *house. For the roof and dark trees in the background the card was very wet and full of paint.*

New Horizons

The use of gouache paint to make a drawing is not an attempt to introduce you to painting, although I would be surprised if you were not interested in doing that as well as drawing. Merely it illustrates a point I have already made, that you should feel free to draw with whatever takes your fancy. An artist cannot be limited by notions of what is proper for him or her to use as a medium. Ultimately the choice is yours. When exercising this choice, try to be inquisitive and adventurous. Any use of a new medium will help your drawing, because it makes you re-assess how you actually produce the finished article. Never use only one medium, even if you prefer it over all others. Your life as an artist is an ever-expanding view of the universe, and if you stick with only one or a select few you will find your artistic horizons narrowing and your work becoming predictable and repetitive. Don't be afraid of what you don't know. Once you start working with a new medium you will be surprised how quickly you appreciate its qualities and find ways of adapting them to your purpose.

SILVER-POINT TECHNIQUE

The last and probably for most people the least likely technique to be attempted is silver-point drawing, the classic method used in the times before pencils were invented. Many drawings by Renaissance artists were made in this way. Anybody interested in producing very precise drawings should try this most refined and effective technique.

First you have to buy a piece of silver wire (try a jeweller or someone who deals in precious metals) about a millimetre thick and about three inches long. This is either held in a wooden handle taped to it or – the better option – within a clutch-action propelling pencil that takes wire of this thickness. Then you cover a piece of cartridge paper (use fairly thick paper because it is less likely to buckle) with a wash of permanent white gouache designer paint; the coat must cover the whole surface and mustn't be either too thick or too watery. When the white paint has dried, you draw onto it with the silver wire; ensure that the end of the wire is smooth and rounded to prevent it tearing the paper. Don't press too hard. The silver deposits a very fine silky line, like a pencil, but lasts much longer. Silver point is a very nice material to draw with. I thoroughly recommend that you make the effort to try it. It's very rewarding as well as instructive.

Joanna B.   Barringham Barber

To use silver point you need to prepare a background to draw onto. I drew this example onto white paint with a bit of reddish-brown mixed in.

Art Appreciation

There are other ways to improve your drawing abilities apart from practising. One approach that is rather pleasurable as well as instructive is to go to as many exhibitions of drawings and paintings as you can. Even if it means travelling a fair distance, this is very worthwhile. Not only does it widen your education in art by making you familiar with first-rate artists, but you will also begin to refine your own perceptions, finding higher levels to aim for in your own work. I myself visit Italy every year to show people around the great works of art in places such as Florence, Venice, Rome and Naples and always find the stimulation very useful for my own work. But don't only look at work by historic masters. Also make the attempt to visit galleries that show the work of current artists, because it is always very instructive to see what your contemporaries are doing and often fuels your own ideas for new directions in your own work.

By your practice of drawing and this appreciation of the art around you, you will experience a measurable upgrading of your own perceptions and understanding of the possibilities at your disposal. This can be great fun as well as uplifting. In any country there are large urban centres where the nation's art is gathered for the public to view, but also you find small colonies of artists tucked away in all sorts of small towns and villages, and their work is worth looking out. Finally, of course, prints and books are very good sources of art appreciation. If you can't afford to buy them, there are vast libraries full of them where they can be studied for free.

WHAT DO YOU SEE?

When viewing the work of other artists, try to analyze what makes it so attractive to you. Ask yourself questions. Don't be ashamed or coy if some of your answers suggest that your response is of a religious or spiritual nature. These are often the truest reasons why we like a work and should be acknowledged. Whatever the chord that is struck when you perceive a work, recognition of it will lead you towards understanding your own work and the direction it might take.

There is room for all sorts of artists in this world and one of the great freedoms of modern art practitioners is that they have completely redefined the reasons behind art. They may not be right, or you may not agree with them, but the freedom to find your own way towards art appreciation is of tremendous value.

When looking at art, question your own perceptions. Is it the subject matter? Is it the technical brilliance of the artist? Is it the colour? Is it the form? Is it the medium used to produce the work? Is it the subtler ideas behind the form? Is it because it reminds you of someone? All these questions are valid. Many more will undoubtedly occur to you. The main point is to discover your true response to a picture that attracts you. Sometimes the answer is very simple, but sometimes the appreciation lies much deeper within yourself and will take some unearthing. Persevere and your reward will be considerable.

Don't try to look at everything. Wait until something really arouses your attention, and then give it your full attention. Spend at least three minutes just looking in detail at everything in the picture, without commenting. Then your questioning of what is in front of you will be very useful in clarifying your understanding.

When looking at reproductions of famous works, notice where these works are held. If it is somewhere near enough for you to visit, do so. No matter how good the quality of a reproduction, the original possesses an extra dimension, and this will leap out at you as soon as you set eyes on the actual work. It is rather like discovering an old friend and seeing them totally afresh. First-hand knowledge of an original also helps to inform you of what is missing when you try to draw from a print of it. Without that knowledge you could not begin to make up for the lack.

ENGAGING WITH LIFE

We have now come full circle. Good art contains an essential ingredient that has to be experienced directly from the work. For this ingredient to be present the artist himself almost certainly must have direct experience of what he is communicating. Drawing from life is therefore of paramount importance. When faced with real people, animals, objects, landscapes, townscapes, whatever, the artist has to assess and then render shape, proportion, tonal variation, perspective and anatomy without losing the verisimilitude of the experience. Obviously, there is some simplification and selection of what is exactly seen. Even so, this is a pretty tall order, and it is because talented artists try to do this all the time that their work is so good. Never forget: drawing from life will increase your ability to draw well. Drawing from drawings or photographs, or making up out of your head are valid, but if you don't return often to the natural visible world your drawings will never be convincing. Quite apart from the benefits it confers, it is the most interesting way to draw, and interest is what keeps art fresh and alive, both for the artist and the viewer.